SPARRING WITH LOVE

A Humorous Guide to Arguing With Your Partner
Without Packing Your Bags

AVERY WELLS

Contents

Introduction

Arguments: we all have them. Whether it's about who left the toothpaste cap off (again) or the deeper, "Why don't you understand me?" conflicts, disagreements are as much a part of relationships as love itself. But don't worry—this isn't a book about eliminating arguments. Frankly, that's impossible unless one of you gets replaced by a robot programmed only to agree. And even then, you'd argue about which model to buy.

The truth is, arguments are a natural (and dare we say, necessary) part of any relationship. They're not just petty squabbles or emotional outbursts; they're opportunities to learn more about each other. Think of them as growing pains for your partnership—uncomfortable but essential for growth. Without them, how would you ever know that your partner is emotionally invested enough to care deeply about your shared Netflix queue?

That said, arguing effectively is an art form. Done poorly, it can escalate from a simple disagreement about the thermostat to a dramatic standoff involving icy silences and passive-aggressive fridge notes. But done well, arguments can help you understand your partner's needs, articulate your own, and build a stronger foundation. They can even be a source of humor—because honestly, have you ever stopped mid-argument to realize how absurd it is to be shouting, "No, you love the dog more than I do!"?

This book is your guide to navigating the messiness of relationship arguments while keeping the love intact (most of the time). Here's the thing: arguing is a skill. It's not about "winning" or "losing," but about learning how to communicate better and, more importantly, love each other through the bumps.

We'll tackle everything from identifying your argument style to mastering the perfect apology, with practical advice and plenty of laughs along the way. Each chapter will offer tools for better communication, sprinkled with humor and lighthearted examples that remind you not to take yourself—or your arguments—too seriously.

By the end of this book, you'll know how to argue like pros, love like fools, and maybe even laugh while doing it. Because, as it turns out, love isn't about never fighting—it's about fighting for each other, even when the going gets tough.

Now, let's dive in and figure out how to make your arguments more constructive, less destructive, and maybe even enjoyable (yes, really).

ONE

Identifying Your Argument Style

L et's face it: arguing with your partner is like attending a dance class where neither of you knows the steps. One of you is doing the cha-cha, the other is attempting a waltz, and somehow, both of you end up stepping on toes. But here's the thing—just like dancing, arguments have styles. The key to getting better at them is figuring out what your style is and how it pairs with your partner's.

Do you clam up and storm off like an Oscar-worthy drama queen? Or are you the type who can't stop talking until your point has been beaten into the ground? (No judgment. Well, maybe a little.) Whatever your approach, understanding your unique argument persona is the first step toward turning those messy missteps into something a little closer to a synchronized routine.

The Silent Stomper, The Over-Talker, The Logical Debater

Let's start with **The Silent Stomper.** Silent Stompers don't argue with words; they argue with actions. Doors are slammed, dishes are put away with a little too much vigor, and there's a lot of sighing—

loud, deliberate sighing. Their goal? To make their partner *feel* their frustration. If you've ever angrily folded laundry, hoping the creases in the towels would somehow communicate your anger, you're a Silent Stomper.

The Silent Stomper's strength lies in their ability to create guilt out of thin air. Their weakness? Communication. Stompers assume their partner knows exactly why they're upset, which is rarely true. The truth is, sulking doesn't translate to problem-solving. If this is you, try saying, "I need space to calm down." A little clarity goes a long way.

Next, we have **The Over-Talker.** Over-Talkers don't just argue—they host a one-person podcast. Their strategy is simple: explain, rephrase, and repeat until their partner caves. Over-Talkers genuinely believe that if they keep talking, their partner will finally see their brilliance. Spoiler: that rarely happens.

For Over-Talkers, the biggest challenge is learning to pause. Conversations are better when they're not one-sided. If you're an Over-Talker, practice saying, "What's your take?" or simply pausing after making your point. It'll feel unnatural at first—like wearing pants that are one size too tight—but over time, you'll realize the magic of listening.

Finally, let's talk about **The Logical Debater.** Logical Debaters approach arguments like courtroom battles. They're armed with evidence, data, and a calm demeanor that somehow makes you feel like you've already lost. Their mantra is, "I'm not emotional—I'm rational." The problem? Relationships aren't rational.

For example, you might be technically correct that it's not *your fault* the milk was left out, but that doesn't erase your partner's frustration when they pour curdled cream into their coffee. Logical Debaters are great at winning arguments but often miss the bigger picture: being right isn't the same as being kind. If this is you, remember that sometimes your partner doesn't want a solution—they just want to feel understood.

Of course, many of us don't fit neatly into one category. You might be a Silent Stomper during emotional fights but an Over-Talker when discussing finances. Or maybe you start as a Logical Debater, then devolve into stomping when the stakes get personal. Understanding these shifts is key to improving your conflict skills.

Mismatched styles can lead to hilariously predictable clashes. A Silent Stomper paired with an Over-Talker is like watching an unstoppable force meet an immovable object. One person retreats, while the other follows, delivering a monologue that echoes through the halls. Similarly, a Logical Debater and an Over-Talker might find themselves locked in an endless spiral of logic and words, with neither willing to yield. These patterns are frustrating—but also a little funny when you step back and notice them.

So, what's the solution? Step one is recognizing your style and your partner's. Step two is adjusting. Silent Stompers, try saying, "I'll be back in a minute," instead of slamming the door. Over-Talkers, practice silence—it won't kill you. Logical Debaters, stop trying to win every argument with bulletproof reasoning; sometimes an "I hear you" is more valuable than a flowchart.

Learning your argument style isn't about assigning blame. It's about gaining self-awareness and building bridges with your partner. Because at the end of the day, arguments aren't about being perfect —they're about progress.

How to Recognize and Respect Each Other's Style

Recognizing your partner's argument style is like identifying different birds at the park. Silent Stompers are like swans—elegantly retreating, but there's rage behind those calm exteriors. Over-Talkers are parrots, squawking endlessly until you hear their point. Logical

Debaters? They're the owls, perched high with facts and wisdom, but maybe just a bit too aloof. Learning to respect these styles is key to surviving—and thriving—through your disagreements.

The first step is understanding what's happening beneath the surface. A Silent Stomper doesn't stomp away because they want to win the "Most Dramatic Exit" award. Usually, they're overwhelmed and need space to process. Think of their stomping as an emotional buffering period. Respecting their style means giving them the room they need without chasing after them shouting, "We're not done here!" Instead, try saying something simple, like, "I get that you need a break. Let's talk when you're ready." Bonus points if you resist the urge to slam a door yourself.

Over-Talkers are a different challenge. They genuinely believe that if they explain their feelings just one more time, the light bulb will finally go off for you. Their superpower is their persistence; their kryptonite is knowing when to stop. If you're paired with one, you've probably mastered the art of nodding politely while tuning them out at minute twenty. But respect works both ways. Instead of zoning out, try gently interjecting with humor: "I'm going to need a snack break if this explanation gets any longer." For Over-Talkers themselves, respecting others' styles means pausing—yes, pausing— to let their partner speak. Trust me, silence won't kill you.

Logical Debaters are a breed all their own. They love facts, structure, and airtight arguments. If you've ever felt like you were in court during a fight, congratulations—you're with a Debater. While their rational approach can be useful, it often makes emotional partners feel dismissed. Respecting a Logical Debater means acknowledging their points, even if you disagree. Try saying, "I get where you're coming from, but I need you to understand how this makes me feel." Logical Debaters, in turn, need to step out of their spreadsheets and say things like, "That sucks. I'm sorry," without needing to cite a source.

Sometimes, these styles clash in ways that are just plain funny. Picture a Silent Stomper paired with an Over-Talker. One storms off, and the other follows, delivering a heartfelt TED Talk on the way to the next room. Or imagine two Logical Debaters going head-to-head. That's not an argument—it's a dissertation defense. When you step back and see how ridiculous these interactions can be, it's easier to stop taking them so seriously.

The key to respecting each other's style is simple: assume good intentions. Your Silent Stomper isn't trying to frustrate you; they're just processing. Your Over-Talker isn't trying to drown you in words; they're trying to connect. And your Logical Debater isn't trying to turn your relationship into a courtroom; they're just looking for fairness. When you stop interpreting their behavior as a personal attack, you can start finding humor in their quirks.

Adjustments also help. Silent Stompers can learn to say, "I need a moment, but I'll come back," instead of disappearing in a huff. Over-Talkers can practice pausing after each point, even if it feels awkward. Logical Debaters can remind themselves that not everything needs to be solved with a pie chart. Small tweaks go a long way.

Finally, laugh together. Humor is a relationship superglue, and nothing disarms tension faster than being able to chuckle at yourselves. Call each other out lovingly: "Oh, look, The Great Stomper has entered the kitchen," or "Here comes a PowerPoint presentation from Dr. Data." These moments of levity remind you that you're a team, not adversaries.

When you learn to recognize and respect each other's argument styles, disagreements become less about "winning" and more about understanding. And that's the real victory. Speaking of which, next we'll talk about breaking patterns and improving communication—because even the best of us repeat the same fights if we're not careful.

Tips for Identifying Patterns and Improving Communication

Arguments in relationships often feel like reruns. Sure, the topic changes—dishes one day, forgotten plans the next—but the script stays eerily similar. That's because most fights aren't about what's on the surface. They're about patterns. Identifying those patterns is like unlocking a secret map to your relationship. It doesn't mean you'll never argue again, but it does help you navigate disagreements with less drama.

The first step is spotting your common triggers. Do you argue more at certain times? Maybe tensions spike after a long day at work or during particularly stressful weeks. Or maybe one of you is not a morning person, while the other can't resist launching into a deep discussion before the coffee's even brewed. Recognizing these triggers can help you pause before diving headfirst into a familiar fight.

Next, look for recurring themes. Do your arguments about chores usually boil down to one partner feeling underappreciated? Or does every money fight lead to fears about security? These deeper issues fuel the arguments, like an undercurrent you can't always see. By identifying these themes, you can address the root problem rather than repeatedly arguing over symptoms.

But patterns aren't just about *what* you fight about—they're in *how* you fight, too. Maybe one of you shuts down at the first sign of conflict, leaving the other to fill the silence. Or perhaps one of you always goes on the defensive, turning every disagreement into a battle of egos. Pay attention to how your fights usually play out. Do you interrupt? Escalate? Play the blame game? Recognizing these habits is the first step to breaking the cycle.

Once you've noticed these patterns, the next step is sharing your observations—but timing matters. The middle of a heated argument is not the moment to bring this up. Instead, pick a neutral, calm time, like over dinner or during a weekend walk. Use "we" statements to avoid blame. For instance, "I think we argue more when we're tired," is much less likely to spark defensiveness than, "You're always cranky and start fights."

Here's another tip: swap blame for curiosity. Instead of accusing your partner of being difficult, try asking, "What's making this feel so important to you?" This simple shift can turn an argument into a conversation. It also shows your partner that you care about their perspective, not just proving your own point.

Active listening is another game-changer. It sounds easy, but in the heat of an argument, it's surprisingly hard to do. Active listening means focusing entirely on what your partner is saying without planning your next counterpoint. Nod, repeat back key ideas, and ask questions like, "Can you explain what you mean?" Even if you disagree, making your partner feel heard can defuse tension almost instantly.

Don't forget about setting small, achievable goals during arguments. Instead of trying to fix everything at once, focus on making progress in one area. For example, if you're fighting about money, don't try to overhaul your entire budget mid-argument. Instead, agree on one small step, like reviewing expenses together later. Small wins build momentum and help you feel like a team, even when tensions are high.

And then there's humor—your secret weapon. A well-timed joke can diffuse even the most heated arguments. Let's say you're mid-fight about laundry. Throw in, "Maybe the dryer ate my common sense along with all those socks." Laughter can break the tension and remind you both that you're on the same side. Of course, timing is key. Don't joke if your partner is in full rage mode—save it for when the steam starts to cool.

Ultimately, identifying patterns and improving communication isn't about avoiding arguments altogether—it's about learning to argue better. When you can recognize your triggers, address the real issues, and communicate with respect, arguments become less destructive and more productive. And if you can laugh a little along the way, even better.

Speaking of productive arguments, the next step is setting ground rules for fair fighting—because every great fight needs boundaries.

Humor About Classic Argument Behaviors and What They Reveal

Arguments are like reality TV: entertaining when it's someone else, but exhausting when it's you. The funny thing is, our argument behaviors—while frustrating—reveal a lot about who we are. And when you step back and look at them objectively, they're kind of hilarious. Let's dig into some of the classics and what they secretly say about us.

First up, **The Door Slammer.** This person doesn't just leave the room—they make an *exit.* The slam is their punctuation mark, their mic drop, their declaration of "Conversation over!" without saying a word. What does this behavior reveal? Door Slammers thrive on drama. They want their feelings to be noticed, preferably with an echo. It's not that they're trying to destroy the doorframe; they just want their partner to realize, *right now,* how upset they are.

On the opposite end is **The Note Leaver.** This person avoids confrontation by leaving passive-aggressive Post-its. "Please rinse the dishes before putting them in the sink" or "Apparently, the laundry doesn't fold itself." What does this reveal? Note Leavers hate conflict but love control. They dream of a world where their requests are fulfilled without uttering a word. Deep down, they know the note won't work, but it feels oddly satisfying to leave it anyway.

Then there's **The Interrupter.** This person can't wait their turn. They'll cut you off mid-sentence with, "That's not true!" or, "Wait, let me explain!" What does this reveal? Interrupters are debate champions at heart. They care so much about their point that they jump in before hearing yours. It's not that they don't respect you—it's that they think the conversation will end if they don't get their thoughts out immediately.

We can't forget **The Over-Explainer.** This is the person who starts with, "Here's why I'm upset," and doesn't stop until they've outlined every detail. Their partner usually zones out somewhere around "Chapter Two: Why You Left the Milk Out." What does this reveal? Over-Explainers are terrified of being misunderstood. Their motto is, "If I explain this thoroughly enough, you'll get it." Spoiler: their partner rarely gets it by the end of the monologue.

The Silent Treatment Specialist is next. This person weaponizes quiet, wielding their silence like a sword. They might sulk for hours —or days—waiting for their partner to decode the message behind the silence. What does this reveal? Silent Treatment Specialists aren't heartless; they're overwhelmed. For them, silence is a way to avoid saying something regrettable, but it leaves their partner guessing.

On a lighter note, there's **The Compliment Fighter.** This person starts an argument but then says things like, "It's annoying, but you're cute when you're mad," or, "I can't stay mad at you." What does this reveal? Compliment Fighters are charmers who'd rather diffuse tension than face it head-on. They hope a little flirting will erase the problem. It works... sometimes.

Last but not least, we have **The Dramatic Hypotheticalist.** This person loves throwing out wild scenarios. "If I disappeared, would you even notice?" or, "What if I just quit my job and became a llama farmer—would that make you happy?" What does this reveal? They're not serious about llamas. Instead, they're fishing for reassurance. They want their partner to say, "Of course I'd notice. I'd miss you."

These behaviors, as maddening as they are in the moment, are also oddly human. They're different ways of expressing what we all want: to be seen and understood. Yes, they're frustrating, but they're also funny when you look back at them. The next time your partner slams a door or leaves a Post-it note about socks, take a moment to breathe and laugh. Behind every dramatic hypothetical and overlong explanation is a person just trying to connect—however clumsily.

Speaking of clumsy, the *timing* of arguments can make or break them. In the next chapter, we'll dive into why knowing when to argue is as important as knowing how.

TWO

Setting Ground Rules for Fair Fighting

Arguments without rules are like board games without instructions—chaotic, confusing, and likely to end with someone flipping the table. When it comes to disagreements in relationships, setting some ground rules isn't just helpful; it's essential. It's what separates a healthy debate from an all-out emotional brawl.

Think of these rules as your relationship's safety net. They're not there to stop arguments from happening—because let's be honest, that's impossible—but to make sure things don't spiral into hurt feelings, slammed doors, or someone angrily eating the last slice of pizza out of spite. A few clear boundaries can keep your fights productive, respectful, and (dare I say) even a little bit loving.

In this chapter, we'll explore the golden rules for fair fighting. From avoiding low blows to knowing when to take a time-out, these tips will help you and your partner tackle conflict without feeling like you're starring in an episode of *Real Couples of Passive Aggression*. So grab a metaphorical whistle, and let's learn how to referee your arguments like pros.

Creating "Fair Fight" Rules Like No Bringing Up Old Arguments

Arguments in relationships are inevitable, but without rules, they can quickly turn into emotional cage matches where nobody wins and everyone leaves bruised. That's where fair fight rules come in—they're the secret sauce that keeps disagreements productive, respectful, and (dare I say) survivable. The first and arguably most important rule? **No bringing up old arguments.**

Why is this rule so crucial? Because resurrecting old fights is like digging up a zombie—unnecessary, messy, and destined to cause more chaos than you bargained for. You think you're just reminding your partner about that "one time," but what you're really doing is steering the current argument off a cliff and into a pit of unresolved grievances. Suddenly, you're not just talking about today's issue—you're relitigating an argument from 2017 about who forgot to bring the sunscreen on vacation.

Let's be honest: we all love the temptation of a good "Remember when...?" moment. It's your brain's way of saying, "Hey, if I can prove they were wrong before, it strengthens my case now!" But while it feels satisfying in the moment, it's about as helpful as throwing gasoline on a campfire. Not only does it escalate the argument, but it also shifts the focus from solving the current problem to rehashing the past.

So how do you avoid bringing up old arguments? First, learn to recognize when you're about to do it. You'll hear that little voice in your head whisper, "This is the perfect time to remind them they were late to your cousin's wedding!" Don't listen to that voice. Instead, pause and ask yourself: *Will this help us solve the current issue or just make things worse?* If it's the latter, let it go. Better yet, imagine a giant, neon mental sign that says: "No Dead Arguments Beyond This Point."

But what if your partner is the one who keeps dragging old skeletons into the argument? Try humor to defuse the moment. When they start down the "greatest hits of grievances" road, you can jokingly say, "Oh, we're playing the classics today, huh?" It's a lighthearted way to point out the derailment without adding fuel to the fire.

This rule isn't about pretending the past doesn't matter; it's about separating old issues from new ones. If there's an unresolved problem that keeps creeping into your fights, address it directly when you're both calm. Schedule a conversation to hash it out once and for all. Say something like, "I've noticed we keep circling back to this. Can we talk about it and put it to rest?" That's a lot healthier (and more productive) than throwing it into every disagreement like a grenade.

Of course, this rule also requires teamwork. Both partners have to commit to leaving past arguments where they belong—in the past. It helps to set clear boundaries, like agreeing that once an issue is resolved, it stays resolved. No sneak attacks. No surprise "remember when" ambushes. Trust me, your relationship will thank you.

And because every rule benefits from a little levity, don't be afraid to poke fun at yourselves. Maybe you create a "no past argument jar," where every time someone brings up an old fight, they have to toss in a dollar. Or keep a running joke about how many months it's been since the last mention of "the great dishwasher debate of 2021." Laughter isn't a cure-all, but it sure makes the hard stuff easier to navigate.

The truth is, letting go of past fights isn't just about fairness—it's about freedom. It frees you from carrying resentment, frees your partner from feeling like they're perpetually on trial, and frees your relationship from the weight of old mistakes. Because at the end of the day, the goal isn't to "win" every fight; it's to build a partnership where you both feel valued, respected, and safe.

And speaking of respect, the next rule is all about keeping arguments free of harsh words. Let's explore how to disagree without accidentally turning your partner into an emotional punching bag.

How to Keep Arguments Respectful Without Harsh Words

Arguments have a way of escalating from "I feel unheard" to "You're impossible!" in under a minute. That's why keeping things respectful—even when you're mad enough to scream—is critical. Harsh words might feel satisfying in the moment, but they leave a mess no one wants to clean up.

So why do harsh words slip out? Frustration is usually the culprit. You've repeated yourself three times, your partner still doesn't get it, and suddenly, instead of saying, "I need you to hear me," you snap, "You never listen, and you're so selfish!" It's a verbal grenade, and while it feels powerful, it only leaves rubble in its wake.

Defensiveness is another culprit. When your partner points out a mistake, it's tempting to retaliate with, "Oh, I'm messy? At least I'm not the one who leaves dirty dishes for days!" Congratulations— you've sidestepped the issue *and* thrown gasoline on the fire.

The problem with harsh words is that they stick. Long after the fight is over, you might forget what started it, but you'll remember being called "lazy" or "selfish." These labels plant seeds of resentment, and over time, those seeds grow into walls between you and your partner.

The first step to keeping things respectful? **Ban name-calling.** Sure, it feels justified in the moment, but calling your partner "irresponsible" or "a control freak" isn't going to win you any points. Focus on the behavior, not the person. Saying, "I feel frustrated when the bills aren't paid on time," is much better than, "You're terrible with money." One invites conversation; the other slams the door.

Another tip: **Pause before speaking.** When emotions run high, it's easy to let words fly before thinking. Taking a moment to breathe—literally—can help you choose better words. If you're unsure what to say, try something neutral, like, "I need a second to think about how to respond." It's awkward but much better than, "You're just like your mother."

"I" statements are another lifesaver. Instead of saying, "You never help around the house," try, "I feel overwhelmed when I don't have help with chores." It shifts the focus from blame to your feelings, which makes it less likely your partner will get defensive. A small change, but a big difference.

Know when to call a time-out. Arguments can snowball quickly, especially when voices get louder and patience runs thin. If you feel things escalating, say, "I don't want this to get out of hand. Can we take a break and come back to it later?" Just make sure you revisit the issue once you're both calmer. A time-out isn't an escape hatch—it's a pause button.

Lastly, don't underestimate the power of humor. A well-timed joke can break tension and remind you both that you're on the same team. If your partner accuses you of leaving socks everywhere, you could reply, "I'm marking my territory, like a very confused dog." It won't solve the problem, but it might make you both laugh—and that's a start.

Keeping arguments respectful isn't about avoiding conflict. It's about expressing yourself in a way that your partner can actually hear. When you ditch the harsh words, focus on your feelings, and throw in a little humor, fights become less about destruction and more about connection. And that's the real goal, right?

Now that we've mastered respect, let's tackle the art of compromise—because finding middle ground is easier said than done.

Tips for Finding Compromise Even During Disagreements

Compromise is the unicorn of arguments: hard to find, and occasionally you wonder if it's even real. But in relationships, it's essential. The goal isn't to let one person "win" while the other sulks into the couch cushions; it's about finding that sweet spot where both of you feel like you got enough to stop glaring at each other.

Step one: **Realize you won't always get everything you want.** Harsh, I know, but that's life. If you insist on sushi but your partner demands pizza, compromise might mean alternating dinner choices or choosing tacos instead—because tacos are Switzerland: neutral, delicious, and impossible to argue about.

Step two: **Pick your battles.** Not every disagreement needs to turn into a hill you're ready to die on. If you find yourself arguing over whether to fold towels in thirds or halves, it's time to ask, "Is this really worth the energy?" Spoiler: it's not. Save your fight fuel for bigger issues, like whether to adopt a dog or a cat—or what to name the dog when you win that fight.

Step three: **Be clear about your needs.** Saying, "I wish you'd help more" is too vague to work. Instead, try something specific, like, "Can you do the dishes on Thursdays?" This gives your partner something concrete to work with—and prevents the dreaded, "I didn't know what you meant!" excuse.

Step four: **Actually listen to each other.** Shocking, right? Instead of treating the argument like a courtroom where you're the lead prosecutor, try asking, "What would work for you?" Then, resist the urge to scoff if their solution involves eating dinner at 4 p.m. or installing four separate remotes for the TV. Listening doesn't mean agreeing—it just means understanding.

Step five: **Get creative.** If you can't agree on one solution, brainstorm together. You want a weekend getaway, but your partner wants to stay home? Suggest a day trip. You want action movies, and they want rom-coms? Watch an action-comedy. It's not about splitting everything perfectly—it's about finding something that feels fun instead of forced.

Step six: **Let go of your ego.** Compromise often gets stuck because someone refuses to "lose." But here's the secret: compromise isn't losing. It's choosing happiness over stubbornness. There's no award for Most Victorious Partner (and if there were, would it even be worth it?).

Step seven: **Celebrate small wins.** When your partner meets you halfway, show some appreciation. Say, "Thanks for going with my idea," or, "I know this wasn't your first choice, and I appreciate it." Gratitude softens resistance and makes future compromises easier.

Step eight: **Use humor.** Laughter doesn't fix arguments, but it makes them less painful. If you're stuck in a stalemate, try something like, "Flip a coin? Or should we settle this with rock-paper-scissors?" Joking reminds you both that you're on the same team, even if it doesn't feel like it in the moment.

Compromise isn't about one person giving everything up. It's about finding a balance where both of you feel respected. Sure, it might mean watching your partner's favorite show instead of yours, or trying that vegan restaurant even if you're skeptical about chickpea burgers. But in the end, it's less about what you give up and more about what you gain—a partner who feels valued, a relationship that grows stronger, and maybe even an appreciation for rom-coms. (Maybe.)

Now that we've cracked the code to compromise, let's dive into some lighthearted examples of how to create ground rules for fighting fairly —and actually stick to them.

Lighthearted Examples of Common "Ground Rules" That Help

Ground rules for arguments are like safety rails on a roller coaster—they won't stop the twists and turns, but they'll keep you from flying off the track. While every couple's rules might look a little different, the best ones share a common goal: ensuring your fights stay fair, respectful, and (when possible) a little less miserable.

Let's start with a classic: **"No fighting before coffee."** This rule is a lifesaver for anyone who isn't a morning person. Nothing good ever comes from discussing serious topics before caffeine has entered the bloodstream. Want to talk about the budget or why there's a wet towel on the bed? Wait until after breakfast. Bonus: this rule buys you time to think through your points instead of blurting out, "Why are you like this?" before the toaster even pops.

Next up: **"Take turns talking."** Sounds obvious, right? But when emotions are running high, it's tempting to interrupt with, "That's not what happened!" or, "Let me just correct that." The result? Chaos. Agreeing to let each person finish their thought might feel like torture if you're dying to respond, but it ensures both of you feel heard—and less like you're on a game show where the loudest contestant wins.

Then there's the trusty **"Time-out rule."** This one's for when arguments start to spiral. If voices are rising and tempers are flaring, either person can call a time-out. The catch? Time-outs aren't escapes. You have to return to the conversation after cooling down—preferably without slamming a door, though dramatic exits can be forgiven if they're followed by an actual resolution.

Here's a fun one: **"No fighting in public."** Ever had an argument in front of friends or family? It's awkward for everyone involved, especially your audience, who are suddenly torn between pretending they didn't hear anything or awkwardly changing the subject to the weather. Make a pact to save disagreements for when you're alone. Your friends (and your dignity) will thank you.

Another helpful rule: **"No phones during fights."** The only thing worse than a heated argument is one where your partner is scrolling Instagram while you're making your case. Banishing phones during disagreements keeps both of you present—and avoids the accidental rage spiral of, "Did you just 'like' a meme while I was talking?"

For couples who are prone to escalating, consider the **"Volume check rule."** If one of you notices things getting too loud, agree to lower your voices. Yelling might feel cathartic, but it rarely solves anything—unless the argument is about who can shout the loudest, in which case, congratulations on the weirdest competition ever.

The **"Do not weaponize old arguments"** rule is non-negotiable. We've all been tempted to play the greatest hits: "Remember the time you ruined dinner by using salt instead of sugar?" or, "What about the 2018 vacation fiasco?" But bringing up old fights is like throwing expired milk into the mix—it's gross, unhelpful, and leaves everyone feeling sour. Keep the focus on the current disagreement, not a scrapbook of past mistakes.

Finally, try the **"End with something positive"** rule. Even if the argument isn't resolved, take a moment to remind each other that you're on the same team. A simple "I'm frustrated, but I love you" can go a long way toward softening hard feelings. It's cheesy, yes, but it works. Plus, it ensures you're not going to bed with someone plotting a revenge snore.

These ground rules aren't just about making arguments less painful—they're about turning them into opportunities to strengthen your relationship. With a few simple agreements, fights become less like a battle for dominance and more like a collaborative effort to understand each other better.

And hey, once you've set the rules, don't forget to laugh at yourselves when you inevitably break one. Humor is the ultimate relationship hack, and a well-timed, "Oops, I just broke the 'no interrupting' rule" can remind both of you why you're doing this: to fight fair, love better, and maybe even argue with a little grace.

In the next chapter, we'll explore why timing matters in arguments—because let's be honest, some fights are doomed from the start if you pick the wrong moment. Let's figure out how to fight smarter by knowing *when* to argue.

THREE

The Power of Timing - Knowing When to Argue

Arguments are like thunderstorms: if they hit at the wrong time, they can wreak havoc. But when timed right? They can clear the air. Unfortunately, most of us don't check the emotional weather forecast before diving into a disagreement. Instead, we pick the absolute worst moments—five minutes before bed, halfway through dinner, or right as someone is stepping into the shower—to launch into, "So we need to talk."

Timing matters. A poorly timed argument is like trying to assemble IKEA furniture at 2 a.m.—you're too tired, too cranky, and no one has the patience to figure out where that missing screw went. If you want your arguments to actually go somewhere (other than straight to Frustrationville), learning *when* to argue is just as important as *how* to argue.

In this chapter, we'll explore the art of timing. From recognizing bad moments to finding the right ones, you'll learn how to avoid the traps that turn minor disagreements into epic blowouts. And who knows? With better timing, you might even find yourself arguing less. Or at least not mid-shower.

Let's get started. (But not right before bed.)

Why Timing Matters for Effective Conflict Resolution

Timing can make or break an argument. Start a serious discussion while your partner is brushing their teeth, and you've already lost. Ambush them during their favorite show's finale? You're now the villain in their narrative. Timing isn't just a convenience—it's a crucial ingredient for resolving disagreements without spiraling into chaos.

Poor timing is counterproductive. Imagine trying to discuss finances right after your partner gets home from a stressful workday. They're mentally exhausted and just want to collapse on the couch, but you've launched into, "We need to talk about our spending." Cue frustration, defensiveness, and a ruined evening. Timing matters because it sets the emotional stage. A calm, receptive partner is much more likely to engage productively than one who's stressed, tired, or hungry.

And then there's the notorious **bedtime ambush.** You're lying in bed, and suddenly your brain decides it's the perfect time to revisit that snarky comment your partner made at brunch three days ago. Spoiler alert: it's not. Late-night arguments are emotional landmines. One of you is trying to sleep, and the other is about to launch into a monologue about feelings. The result? Hurt feelings, restless sleep, and no real resolution.

So how do you fix this? **Learn to recognize bad moments.** If your partner is distracted—scrolling through emails, wrangling kids, or dealing with IKEA instructions—don't pounce. The middle of a chaotic moment isn't the time to bring up why you're upset. Wait for a better opportunity. Think of it like fishing: cast your line at the wrong time, and you'll scare the fish away (or in this case, your partner).

Timing isn't just about them—it's also about you. If you're frazzled, hangry, or emotionally keyed up, step back. Ask yourself, "Am I ready to discuss this calmly, or am I about to yell because I skipped lunch?" Self-awareness is key. Arguing effectively requires a clear head, not one swirling with unresolved work stress and a growling stomach.

Now, what about **finding the right time?** Look for moments when you're both relaxed, not in a hurry, and emotionally available. After dinner, during a calm evening walk, or while you're enjoying coffee together on a weekend morning—these are prime argument times. You're both in a headspace where you can actually engage. Bonus points if snacks are involved; no one wants to argue with someone holding nachos.

Of course, life isn't perfect, and timing doesn't always cooperate. Sometimes you're frustrated and blurt things out at the wrong moment. That's okay—own it. Saying, "I know this isn't the best time, but this is important to me," shows you're aware of the timing issue but still value the discussion. Acknowledging bad timing can help soften the blow.

Another trap to avoid? **Holiday arguments.** Fighting on special occasions is like spilling coffee on a white dress—it leaves a stain that's hard to forget. Do you really want your romantic getaway memories to include a four-hour debate about whose tone was worse in the car? Save disagreements for another day. Holiday memories are supposed to be happy—or at least less awkward.

Timing also means knowing when *not* to argue. Sometimes, letting a moment slide is the better choice. For instance, if your partner is already kicking themselves for forgetting something, piling on with, "You always do this!" doesn't help. Not every problem needs immediate confrontation, especially if it's minor.

Timing doesn't solve all conflicts, but it makes resolution easier. Picking the right moment shows respect for your partner and increases the chances of a productive conversation. It's not just about avoiding fights—it's about choosing the time when your argument can lead to real progress.

Now that we've covered why timing is critical, let's explore how to resist diving into arguments at the wrong moment. After all, patience isn't easy—but it's worth it.

How to Hold Off Arguments Until the Right Moment

We've all felt it: that burning urge to dive into an argument the second something bothers you. Your partner says something snippy, or you spot socks on the floor for the fourth day in a row, and suddenly it feels like the argument *must* happen immediately. But jumping into a disagreement at the wrong time often leads to dramatic exits, hurt feelings, and zero progress. Mastering the art of waiting isn't easy, but it's the secret weapon of conflict resolution.

So why is waiting so hard? Blame frustration. It's impatient and demanding. Frustration convinces you that addressing the issue immediately will make you feel better. Spoiler: it won't. Rushing into an argument doesn't give you a chance to think clearly or approach the issue constructively. Waiting doesn't mean ignoring the problem —it means setting the stage for a better conversation.

The first step is **recognizing your triggers.** If you're someone who tends to leap into a discussion without considering the timing, practice the art of the pause. Take a deep breath, count to five, or hum the chorus of your favorite song in your head. This tiny moment of reflection can help shift your mindset from reactive to rational, giving you a better chance at addressing the issue effectively.

Next, try **scheduling the conversation.** This might feel overly formal, but it works wonders. If you notice your partner is busy, stressed, or simply not in the mood for a serious chat, don't pounce. Instead, say, "Hey, there's something I'd like to talk about later when we're both free. Would that be okay?" This approach eliminates surprise ambushes and gives you both a chance to mentally prepare for the discussion.

Another great tool? **Writing it down.** If you're worried you'll lose the momentum or forget what's bothering you, jot down a note. Something simple, like "Talk about the sock situation," can help you remember your point without feeling like you have to bring it up immediately. Plus, the act of writing it down can release some of the initial tension, giving you space to calm down.

Timing isn't just about your partner; it's about checking in with **your own mood and energy.** Ask yourself, "Am I ready to have this conversation constructively, or am I about to blow up over something small because I'm hangry?" Self-awareness is crucial for conflict resolution. Waiting even 30 minutes can give you clarity and help you approach the conversation with a cooler head.

Of course, not everyone likes to wait. Some partners might push for immediate resolution with, "Why can't we just talk about it now?" If this happens, stay firm but kind. A simple, "I want to discuss this, but I need a little time to gather my thoughts," can reassure them that you're not avoiding the issue—you're just trying to approach it thoughtfully.

For those moments when frustration is too overwhelming, rely on the magic phrase: **"I need a minute."** It's a lifesaver when emotions are running high. Taking a step back—even for five minutes—gives you a chance to regroup and prevents the argument from escalating into a shouting match or the dreaded "who can slam the door louder" contest.

Another benefit of waiting? It often makes arguments shorter. By holding off until you're both calm and ready to engage, you can avoid the tangents, defensiveness, and irrelevant grievances that tend to drag fights out. It's like solving a puzzle with the right pieces in hand rather than trying to force things into place. Waiting ensures that you can address the issue directly, without turning it into an emotional tornado.

Holding off arguments doesn't mean avoiding them. It means giving yourself and your partner the best chance to approach the conversation productively. After all, no one's at their best when they're rushing out the door, halfway through dinner, or mid-Netflix binge.

Now that we've tackled the importance of timing, let's explore how to honor your partner's mood and energy—because knowing when *they're* ready to engage is just as important as knowing when you are.

Recognizing and Honoring Your Partner's Mood and Energy

Have you ever tried to argue with someone who's clearly not in the mood? Maybe they're exhausted, glued to their phone, or still fuming over a traffic jam. Spoiler: it doesn't go well. Honoring your partner's mood and energy is just as important as timing. If one of you isn't ready for the emotional heavy lifting of a serious conversation, even the smallest disagreement can spiral into chaos.

The first step? **Pay attention to their cues.** People usually give off warning signs when they're not ready to talk. Are they unusually quiet, sighing dramatically, or muttering about their day? These are not green lights to dive into, "We need to talk." Bringing up an issue while they're stressed or preoccupied is like trying to install a ceiling fan during a tornado—it's not going to end well.

That said, respecting their mood doesn't mean waiting indefinitely for the "perfect time." Life isn't a movie, and ideal moments are rare. If you've been holding off for weeks, it's time to ask directly: "Is now a good time to discuss this?" If the answer is no, agree on a time that works for both of you. This avoids endless delays while still respecting their energy.

Recognizing your partner's mood is only half the battle. The other half? **Knowing what helps them reset.** Some people recharge by having alone time, while others need connection to feel grounded. If your partner is the solitary type, give them space to decompress before tackling the big conversation. If they unwind by doing something together, suggest an activity like going for a walk or cooking dinner. Starting the discussion after they've recharged creates a much better foundation for productive conversation.

Of course, this works both ways. **Your mood matters, too.** If you're stressed, tired, or one dirty dish away from losing it, hit pause. No one communicates effectively when they're running on fumes. Take a few minutes to calm yourself—whether that means a snack, a walk, or a quick vent to a friend. Starting the discussion from a balanced place can prevent a minor issue from snowballing into a full-blown fight.

But what if your partner seems to avoid tough conversations entirely? If every "not now" turns into "never," it's time to address the avoidance. Try, "I know this isn't your favorite topic, but it's important to me. Can we agree on a time to talk about it?" This shows that while you respect their need for space, the issue can't stay on the back burner forever.

When moods clash—like when you're ready to talk but they're clearly not—patience becomes your best ally. Resist the urge to force the conversation. Instead, try humor to lighten the mood. Say something like, "I can tell you're not up for a debate right now. Should we save this for after dessert?" A little levity can remind both of you that you're on the same team, not opposing forces.

And let's not forget the elephant in the room: **sometimes it's you who isn't ready.** If you're not in the right headspace, don't push yourself. It's okay to say, "I want to discuss this, but I need a little time to gather my thoughts first." This prevents the argument from turning into a knee-jerk reaction session and gives you time to approach the issue constructively.

Honoring mood and energy isn't about avoiding arguments altogether—it's about creating the right conditions for them to be productive. When both of you are in a good place emotionally, disagreements feel less like battles and more like teamwork. And if your timing still misses the mark? A snack break never hurts.

Next, we'll tackle why arguments always seem to happen at the worst possible times—and how to survive them with your sanity intact.

Humor About Arguments That Start at the Worst Times

Arguments have an uncanny knack for popping up at the absolute worst moments. You're rushing out the door, halfway through a family dinner, or finally settling in for a Netflix binge with snacks in hand when it strikes: "We need to talk." Suddenly, the fight takes over, derailing your plans, souring the mood, and leaving the popcorn cold.

Why does this happen? Stress and bad timing go hand in hand. The more chaotic the moment, the more likely one of you is to snap, turning a minor annoyance into a full-blown disagreement. You're juggling bags, keys, and a coffee cup when your partner makes an offhanded comment, and suddenly, you're yelling about whose turn it was to take out the trash—while the coffee spills on your shoe.

One common offender is **the car fight.** It starts innocently: you're heading somewhere, one of you is driving, and the GPS says, "In 500 feet, turn left." Then comes, "Wait, you missed it!" Cue the passive-aggressive sighs or an annoyed, "Why didn't you say something sooner?" Being trapped in a moving vehicle makes things worse. You're physically stuck together with no exit strategy, so the argument keeps escalating until you arrive at your destination—where you now have to smile and act like nothing's wrong.

Another classic is **the pre-event argument.** You're supposed to meet friends or family in ten minutes, and someone says, "Are you wearing that?" What begins as a tiny comment about your outfit spirals into a debate about personal style, thoughtfulness, and whether one of you even cares about the event. By the time you leave, you're late, frazzled, and silently fuming in the car while pretending everything's fine in front of your friends.

Then there's the **holiday showdown.** Nothing says "season's greetings" like a poorly timed disagreement. You're hosting, the turkey's overcooked, and your partner mentions—just casually—that their mom's turkey is never dry. One snippy comment turns into a whispered argument in the kitchen, which quickly becomes a battle about whose family gets more attention during the holidays. The pie hasn't even been served, and the mood is toast.

So how do you stop these badly timed arguments? The first trick is learning to **pause.** Not every disagreement needs to be tackled immediately. If you feel the tension rising at a terrible moment, say something like, "This is important, but can we discuss it later when we're not rushing?" Pausing doesn't erase the issue, but it gives both of you a chance to cool down before it turns into a disaster.

If you can't pause in the heat of the moment, try to **find the humor.** For example, if you've just argued in the car and are now walking into a party, a lighthearted, "That was a fun pre-party warm-up, huh?" can break the tension. Humor reminds you both that this isn't the end of the world—it's just one bad argument in a long line of human imperfections.

Sometimes, though, the fight will happen despite your best efforts. In these cases, **agree to a truce.** Even if you can't fully resolve the issue, acknowledge that now isn't the time. "I don't want this to ruin the day—let's revisit it later" can prevent a minor disagreement from ruining an entire evening. Truces are lifesavers when you're around others, whether it's at a holiday dinner or during a family reunion.

Finally, **reflect after the fact.** Once things have settled, take a moment to think about what triggered the fight and why it happened then. Did stress, exhaustion, or hunger play a role? Recognizing these patterns helps you avoid falling into the same trap next time.

Bad timing in arguments can't always be avoided, but it can be managed. By pausing, laughing at yourselves, and recognizing when a truce is needed, you can turn a poorly timed fight into just another funny story to share later. After all, most arguments aren't about the event itself—they're about learning how to handle the chaos together.

In the next chapter, we'll explore how to really listen during arguments—a skill that can save you from spiraling into misunderstandings and turning every disagreement into a battle for who gets the last word.

FOUR

Listening Without Planning Your Comeback

L et's be honest: how often do you actually listen to your partner during an argument? Not the polite, head-nodding kind of listening where you're secretly thinking, *I can't wait to crush this point.* I mean the kind where you're really paying attention. If your answer is "not often," welcome to the club. Most of us are too busy mentally drafting the perfect counterargument or dusting off our greatest hits of "Why I'm Right and You're Wrong" to hear what's actually being said.

Here's the thing—listening in an argument is not easy. Your brain doesn't want to sit quietly and take in information. It wants to leap into action, ready to defend your honor and deliver that zinger you're sure will make your partner go, "Wow, I never thought of it that way! You're a genius." Spoiler alert: that moment rarely happens. Instead, you both end up feeling unheard, misunderstood, and more annoyed than when you started.

In this chapter, we're tackling the fine art of *actually* listening during arguments. You'll learn how to stop zoning out mid-rant, why repeating back what your partner said isn't just for therapists, and how to resist the urge to finish their sentences (which, by the way, isn't nearly as cute as you think it is). Listening isn't just a nice relationship skill—it's the secret sauce that turns fights into something less miserable and maybe even productive.

Techniques for Truly Hearing Your Partner's Point of View

Listening during an argument is deceptively hard. Sure, you nod, maintain eye contact, and maybe toss in a strategically timed "I see." But let's be real: half the time, you're just waiting for your turn to talk. Truly hearing your partner's point of view, especially when emotions are high, requires more than passive head-bobbing. It demands intention, focus, and a few clever strategies to keep your brain from wandering off.

The first and most essential step is **silence.** No interruptions, no cutting them off mid-sentence with, "That's not what I meant!" Letting your partner finish their thought is crucial—not just for them, but for you. Interrupting sends a clear message: *What I have to say is more important than what you're saying.* Even if you're convinced they're completely wrong, let them finish. Think of it as a courtesy, like letting someone merge into traffic even when you're in a hurry. Frustrating? Sometimes. Necessary? Always.

Once they've finished, move to **active listening.** This is more than just nodding or grunting an occasional "uh-huh." It's about engaging with their words. Try summarizing their point back to them: "So, you're upset because you felt ignored when I was on my phone?" This technique accomplishes two things: it shows you're paying attention and ensures you're on the same page. Plus, it gives you a little extra time to think about how you want to respond.

Next, **ask clarifying questions.** If your partner says, "I feel like you don't care about my opinion," don't jump straight into, "Of course I care!" Instead, ask, "What makes you feel that way?" or, "Can you give me an example?" Questions like these show genuine curiosity and help uncover the root of the issue. You might discover that their frustration isn't about what you said yesterday—it's about something deeper, like feeling unheard in general.

Resist the urge to **fix things immediately.** Many of us are natural problem-solvers, and when our partner shares a frustration, our first instinct is to swoop in with solutions: "You're stressed? Just tell your boss you need time off!" But most people don't want a fix—they want validation. Try, "That sounds frustrating," instead of launching into a five-step plan to overhaul their work-life balance. Validation doesn't solve the problem, but it makes your partner feel supported, which is half the battle.

Don't forget the importance of **body language.** Listening isn't just about what you say—it's about how you present yourself. Slouching on the couch, crossing your arms, or sneaking glances at your phone screams, "I'm not invested in this conversation." Instead, sit up, lean forward slightly, and make consistent eye contact. Nods, small smiles, and encouraging gestures go a long way in showing your partner that you're engaged. Dramatic sighs and eye rolls, however, do not.

If your partner says something that stings—"You're always late," or "You never prioritize me"—resist the urge to snap back. Instead, **pause before responding.** Take a breath and ask yourself, "Is this really about me, or is this about how they're feeling?" Often, their statement is less about attacking you and more about expressing their own emotions. Responding with empathy, like "I didn't realize you felt that way," defuses tension far better than, "Well, you're no picnic either!"

In tense moments, **humor can be a lifesaver.** If things are starting to spiral, a lighthearted comment—delivered at the right time—can break the tension. If your partner says, "You're always distracted!" you could quip, "What? Sorry, I wasn't listening." (Only do this if your partner appreciates humor; if they're on edge, tread carefully!)

Humor can soften the mood, but it's not a free pass to dismiss their concerns.

Finally, remind yourself that **listening doesn't mean agreeing.** You can acknowledge your partner's feelings without immediately surrendering your perspective. The goal isn't to concede defeat—it's to build understanding. When both people feel heard, the conversation shifts from a battle of egos to a shared effort to resolve the issue.

Mastering these listening techniques takes practice, but it's worth the effort. When your partner feels genuinely heard, they're more likely to listen to you in return. It's not magic—it's mutual respect in action.

Next, we'll explore exercises to sharpen your active listening skills and make every conversation more productive—even the tough ones.

Exercises for Active Listening, Even When You Disagree

Active listening isn't something most of us do naturally. During arguments, it's easy to zone out, plan your next move, or jump in with a rebuttal. These exercises are designed to help you genuinely hear your partner—even when you're itching to prove your point.

The Parrot Method

No, you don't have to squawk, but you do need to repeat back what your partner says. If they say, "I feel like you don't help enough around the house," respond with, "So, you feel like I don't help enough around the house?" It might feel a little robotic, but it forces you to actually process their words instead of rushing to defend yourself. Bonus: they'll correct you if you misinterpret, saving you from arguing over something that wasn't even the issue.

The 5-Second Rule

Not about food this time—this rule is about pausing for five seconds after your partner finishes speaking. This brief moment gives you time to think before responding, making it less likely you'll react emotionally or interrupt. Count to five in your head if you need to, but let their words settle before you reply. It's amazing how much calmer conversations feel when you aren't rushing to speak.

The Curiosity Game

Turn the argument into a challenge to learn more. Ask thoughtful questions about what your partner is sharing. Try, "What made you feel that way?" or, "Can you tell me more about what upset you?" This helps you focus on their perspective and shifts the conversation from confrontation to collaboration. Plus, everyone likes being asked questions—it shows you care.

Body Language Bootcamp

Listening isn't just about words. Slouching, crossing your arms, or checking your phone screams "I'm not paying attention." Instead, sit up, lean forward slightly, and make eye contact. Nodding occasionally or saying, "I see," also helps. Mirroring their posture can create a sense of connection. Bonus tip: avoid dramatic sighs—they're more likely to escalate the argument than help resolve it.

The Empathy Test

When your partner shares a feeling, try responding with, "That must feel..." and finish the sentence with something validating. For example, "That must feel exhausting," or, "That must feel frustrating." This technique shows you're engaging with their emotions, not just waiting to argue back. Empathy helps defuse tension and makes them feel understood.

Listening Without Fixing

Sometimes, your partner just wants to be heard, not "fixed." If they're venting about a tough day, resist the urge to offer solutions.

Instead of saying, "You should talk to your boss," try, "That sounds like a lot to deal with." They'll feel supported, not dismissed, and you'll avoid turning the argument into a problem-solving session they didn't ask for.

Use Humor Carefully

If the conversation allows, humor can lighten the mood. For example, if your partner says, "You always forget to do the dishes," you might reply, "You mean I haven't earned 'Dishwasher of the Year' yet?" Done right, humor acknowledges the problem without escalating the tension. But read the room—if they're too upset, save the jokes for later.

The Role-Switch Exercise

This one's challenging but powerful. After your partner shares their perspective, restate it as if you were in their shoes. For example, "If I were you, I'd feel upset that I wasn't being heard." It's tough, especially when you're convinced you're right, but it forces you to truly consider their point of view. And when someone feels understood, they're more likely to listen to your side.

The "Stay Silent" Challenge

This is for the brave. The next time your partner talks, commit to not saying anything until they've completely finished. No interruptions, no rebuttals—just listening. It's harder than it sounds but incredibly effective for defusing arguments. Sometimes, just letting them talk through their thoughts is all they really need.

Practicing these techniques can feel awkward at first, but they're worth it. Active listening isn't about agreeing with everything your partner says—it's about creating an environment where both of you feel heard. With a little effort, you'll turn arguments into meaningful conversations—and maybe even a few laughs.

Next, we'll explore why people zone out during arguments and how to snap back into focus when it happens.

Lighthearted Advice for Avoiding "Zoning Out" in Arguments

Zoning out during an argument is the relationship equivalent of forgetting someone's name while you're mid-conversation. Your partner is explaining why they're upset, and suddenly, you're staring at the wall thinking, *Is that paint eggshell or off-white?* By the time you realize you've tuned out, they're asking, "Well, what do you think?" and you're scrambling for a response that doesn't give away your mental detour.

It's natural—our brains love distractions, especially when emotions are running high. But zoning out during an argument sends the message that you're not interested, even if that's not true. And let's face it: nothing turns a small disagreement into a full-blown war faster than the dreaded, "Are you even listening to me?"

The good news? Staying present doesn't require superhero-level focus. It starts with recognizing when your brain is wandering and gently nudging it back on track. One of the best ways to stay engaged is to treat the argument as a conversation, not a competition. Instead of thinking about what you're going to say next, focus entirely on what your partner is saying. This sounds simple, but it's harder than it looks—especially when their words hit a nerve.

Body language can also help keep you in the moment. Making eye contact and nodding occasionally shows your partner you're paying attention. Just don't overdo it—you're trying to look engaged, not like a bobblehead. And if you're prone to staring at your phone or fiddling with nearby objects, put them out of reach. Physical distractions often lead to mental ones, so the more grounded you are, the better.

When you catch your mind drifting—which it will—it's okay to admit it. Saying, "Sorry, I got a little distracted, can you repeat that?" is far better than pretending you were listening and fumbling your response. Sure, it's awkward, but your honesty shows your partner that you value the conversation enough to refocus. Plus, you'll avoid the embarrassment of responding to something they didn't actually say.

Listening in an argument also means resisting the urge to fix things. When your partner says, "I feel like you're always on your phone," your first instinct might be to defend yourself or offer a solution, like, "I'll stop scrolling after dinner!" But sometimes, they just want to feel heard. Instead of rushing to respond, try saying, "It sounds like you're feeling ignored," or, "I didn't realize it bothered you so much." This validates their feelings and makes them feel understood, which often calms the conversation.

Humor can also be your secret weapon—when used carefully. If the argument is teetering on the edge of absurdity, a lighthearted comment can defuse tension. For instance, if your partner is upset about your laundry habits, you might say, "So, leaving socks everywhere doesn't count as modern art?" Used sparingly, humor reminds you both that not every disagreement has to feel like the end of the world. Just avoid joking about something they take seriously— it's a fine line between "funny" and "you're sleeping on the couch tonight."

If you find it particularly hard to focus, try repeating your partner's key points back to them. For example, if they say, "I feel like I'm the only one cleaning the kitchen," respond with, "You feel like I'm not pitching in with chores." This forces you to listen and helps clarify their perspective. It also gives them a chance to say, "Exactly," or, "No, that's not quite what I meant," which can prevent misunderstandings.

Finally, remember that staying present doesn't mean agreeing. You can validate your partner's feelings without abandoning your own perspective. The goal is to make them feel heard, not to concede defeat. And when both people feel listened to, arguments become less like shouting matches and more like messy but productive conversations.

Learning to stay present during arguments takes practice, but the payoff is worth it. Not only will your partner feel respected, but you'll also avoid those cringe-worthy moments where they ask, "What did I just say?" and you're forced to mumble, "Uh... something about socks?"

Next, we'll explore how to express your side of the story without turning it into a one-person TED Talk.

Humor About Classic Mistakes Like Finishing Their Sentences

Finishing your partner's sentences might seem like a sign of how well you know them, but in practice, it's more like walking into a room and turning off the music mid-song. Even if your intentions are good, it rarely lands the way you hope. Instead of showcasing your connection, it often makes your partner feel interrupted, misunderstood, and just a little bit annoyed.

Picture this: your partner starts to say, "I've been thinking about how we could..." and you jump in with, "Be better about taking out the trash?" Now, instead of continuing their thought, they stop, look at you, and say, "No, that's not what I was going to say." Congratulations—you've just turned a conversation into a guessing game, and you're losing.

The trouble with finishing sentences is that it assumes you know exactly what your partner is thinking. Maybe you've had similar arguments before, or maybe you just can't resist playing mind reader. Either way, this habit is risky. Even if you guess right, your partner doesn't get the satisfaction of expressing themselves. And when you guess wrong? It's like trying to put a square peg in a round hole—frustrating for everyone involved.

This mistake often comes with a side of unintentional condescension. Imagine your partner says, "I feel like you don't..." and you finish with, "Appreciate you enough?" Depending on your tone, this could come across as self-deprecating humor or a passive-aggressive jab. Guess which one they're likely to hear in the heat of the moment?

Let's be fair—your partner has probably done this to you, too. You start explaining why you didn't text them back, and they cut in with, "Because you were too busy?" Suddenly, you're not just explaining—you're defending yourself against their assumption. The original point gets lost, and now you're arguing about how the conversation itself is unfolding. Classic.

So, how do you stop this verbal shortcut from derailing your arguments? Start with patience. Let your partner finish their thought, even if they pause dramatically like they're in a high school play. Those pauses are where their brain is processing, and interrupting only disrupts the flow.

If you catch yourself in the act, own it. A quick "Sorry, I interrupted—please continue" can go a long way in repairing the moment. It shows you're aware of the habit and willing to step back. Plus, it gives your partner a chance to steer the conversation back on track.

Humor is another handy tool, as long as you use it carefully. If they say, "Stop finishing my sentences!" you could reply, "I was just trying to win the 'Best Listener' award." A little lightheartedness can diffuse tension, but timing is everything. If they're too frustrated, save the jokes for later—or risk escalating things.

Here's a trick: focus on truly listening, rather than predicting. Instead of anticipating their next words, try repeating what they've already said. If they start with, "I've been feeling..." you can respond with, "You've been feeling what?" It keeps the ball in their court while showing you're paying attention. Plus, it's much less likely to backfire.

Communication isn't a race. Sure, guessing their words might save a few seconds, but what's the rush? Letting your partner complete their sentences is about more than avoiding arguments—it's about showing respect. It tells them, "Your thoughts matter, and I want to hear them from you."

Classic mistakes like finishing sentences are easy to fall into, but they're also easy to fix. A little patience, a dash of self-awareness, and maybe a touch of humor can turn this habit into an opportunity to connect more deeply.

And speaking of expressing yourself, in the next chapter we'll explore how to share your side of an argument clearly and calmly—without sounding defensive or accidentally making things worse.

FIVE

Expressing Your Side Clearly and Calmly

Sharing your side of an argument should be simple, right? You open your mouth, say what's on your mind, and voilà— problem solved. Except, in reality, it often goes more like this: you start explaining your point, your partner interrupts, you get flustered, and before you know it, you're yelling, "You're not even letting me finish!" Congratulations, your calm explanation has spiraled into an emotional game of verbal dodgeball.

Expressing yourself during an argument is like trying to give directions while driving in a thunderstorm. You're navigating tricky terrain, emotions are running high, and if you're not careful, you'll end up in a ditch—metaphorically, at least. The good news? There are ways to get your point across without veering off the road or accidentally causing a pile-up.

This chapter is all about how to say what you need to say without sounding defensive, accusatory, or like you're auditioning for a soap opera. You'll learn why "I feel" statements are your new best friend, how to keep your emotions in check when you're ready to explode, and why sometimes less is more when it comes to making your case.

Let's tackle how to express yourself in a way that makes your partner actually want to listen—and maybe even agree with you. Wouldn't that be something?

Tips for Sharing Thoughts Without Sounding Accusatory

Expressing yourself in an argument is a delicate art. You want to be honest about how you feel, but the moment it comes out as "You always do this!" your partner's defenses go up faster than you can say, "That's not what I meant." Suddenly, the conversation is no longer about the issue—it's about how you phrased it. Welcome to the communication equivalent of stepping on a rake.

The trick to sharing your thoughts without sounding accusatory lies in one magical phrase: **"I feel."** Instead of pointing fingers with "You never help with the housework," try, "I feel overwhelmed when I handle all the chores alone." Same sentiment, but one frames the problem as a personal feeling, while the other sounds like a judgment. "I feel" statements shift the focus from blame to communication—and best of all, they make your partner less likely to shout, "That's not true!"

But let's not pretend this is easy. When you're upset, "I feel" can feel like an unnatural filter. Your brain wants to blurt out, "You're so inconsiderate!" because it's quick and satisfying. Yet, those words are like verbal dynamite—they might make an impact, but they also leave behind a mess. Taking a deep breath and rephrasing into something like, "I feel hurt when my needs aren't prioritized," keeps the conversation grounded instead of explosive.

Tone is equally important. You could say, "I feel like you don't listen to me," in a way that sounds calm and open, or in a way that makes your partner roll their eyes and think, *Here we go again.* The same words, delivered differently, can either invite a discussion or start a standoff. Keep your tone steady—no sarcasm, no heavy sighs, and definitely no theatrical pauses for effect. Unless you're in a stage play, drama doesn't help.

Another pitfall to avoid? Overloading your sentences with absolutes like "always" and "never." "You never listen to me" is a sure-fire way to turn the discussion into a debate about the one time they did listen six months ago. Instead, try specifics: "It upset me when I didn't feel heard earlier today." Specifics keep the conversation tethered to reality, rather than descending into exaggerated "you're the worst" territory.

Here's a fun challenge: when sharing your thoughts, pretend you're a translator. Your job is to take the raw emotion bubbling up inside you and turn it into words your partner can actually process. Think of it this way: saying "You're impossible!" is like shouting in a language they don't understand. Translating that to "I'm frustrated because I feel like we're not solving this together" makes your feelings clear without shutting down the conversation.

Humor can also be your secret weapon—but only if it's well-timed. For example, if you're upset about who left the car on empty again, you might say, "I feel like my name was accidentally left off the 'gas fairy' schedule." Light humor can disarm tension and open the door to problem-solving. Just be careful not to make jokes at your partner's expense—that's a quick way to turn a light moment into a fight over something completely unrelated.

It's also worth practicing the fine art of **brevity.** When emotions run high, it's tempting to unload every grievance you've ever had. But rattling off a list of complaints doesn't make your point stronger—it makes your partner tune out. Stick to one issue at a time, and save the others for later (or, better yet, let them go if they don't actually matter). A focused discussion is far more effective than a scattershot airing of grievances.

Finally, don't forget to **listen as much as you speak.** Expressing yourself clearly isn't just about what you say—it's about creating space for your partner to respond. If they feel like they're being lectured, they're less likely to engage. Sharing your thoughts without sounding accusatory isn't about dominating the conversation—it's about opening it up.

With a little patience and practice, you can turn those emotional outbursts into thoughtful expressions of what's really on your mind. And once you master sharing your side, the next challenge is staying calm—because delivering your thoughts like a peaceful sage is much harder when you're on the verge of losing it.

Practicing "I Feel" Statements to Reduce Defensiveness

Arguments have a way of escalating fast, especially when one person feels attacked. The quickest way to light that fuse? Start with "You always" or "You never." Nothing makes a partner retreat into defensiveness faster than feeling accused. Enter the humble hero of conflict resolution: the "I feel" statement. It's simple, effective, and, most importantly, makes you sound less like a prosecutor and more like a human being.

At its core, an "I feel" statement is all about taking ownership of your emotions instead of assigning blame. It transforms, "You're so inconsiderate for leaving the dishes again!" into, "I feel overwhelmed when the dishes pile up." The difference? One sparks an argument, and the other invites a conversation. Sure, it might not immediately get the dishes done, but at least it keeps the fight from ending with someone dramatically slamming the silverware drawer.

Here's the thing about "I feel" statements—they're harder than they seem. When you're in the heat of the moment, your brain wants to default to, "Why do you always do this?" because it's quick, satisfying, and feels like the emotional mic drop you're sure will win the argument. Spoiler: it never does. "I feel" statements, on the other hand, take effort. You have to pause, reflect on your feelings, and then find a way to share them without turning them into accusations. It's not as flashy, but it's far more effective.

To make this work, keep your statements simple. "I feel unappreciated when my efforts go unnoticed," is clear and direct. Adding qualifiers like, "because you never say anything nice," drags the focus back to blame. It's like tossing a banana peel on an otherwise clear path—you're just setting yourself up for a slip.

Timing is also key. Dropping an "I feel" statement into a conversation that's already spiraling out of control might not have the desired effect. If voices are raised and tempers are flaring, even the gentlest approach can get lost in the chaos. Instead, wait for a moment of calm, or create one by saying, "Can we take a step back? Here's how I'm feeling." It resets the tone and signals your intent to work together, not fight.

Another pro tip? Pair your "I feel" statement with a clear request. Saying, "I feel frustrated when I'm the only one cleaning up," is a great start, but adding, "Could we split the chores this week?" turns it into actionable communication. You're not just venting—you're offering a solution.

And while we're here, let's talk about the dreaded misuse of "I feel" statements. Some people try to disguise accusations as feelings, like, "I feel like you're selfish." Nice try, but that's just a blame grenade wrapped in soft packaging. A true "I feel" statement focuses on your emotions, not your partner's character flaws. It might take practice, but once you get the hang of it, you'll notice a real difference in how your partner responds.

Humor can also play a role in diffusing tension. If the argument feels heavy, a playful, "I feel like we might need a chore wheel—maybe with glitter?" can bring a smile while still addressing the issue. Just be careful to keep the humor light and directed at the situation, not your partner.

And finally, don't forget to check in with your partner. After sharing your feelings, ask something like, "Does that make sense to you?" or, "How do you feel about what I just said?" This shows that you're not just unloading—you're genuinely interested in their perspective. It shifts the conversation from a one-sided complaint to a collaborative discussion.

Mastering "I feel" statements is a game-changer for reducing defensiveness and opening up better communication. They won't solve every problem, but they'll make it much easier to approach issues as a team. Next, we'll explore how to stay calm and collected when emotions are running high—because delivering your message effectively is even harder when you're on the verge of a meltdown.

Strategies for Staying Calm and Collected

Staying calm during an argument is one of those skills that sounds great in theory but feels impossible in practice. When emotions are running high, staying level-headed can feel like trying to balance a flaming bowling pin on your nose. But if you can master the art of staying calm, you'll not only make your point more effectively, but you'll also keep the argument from spiraling into the dreaded no-man's-land of hurt feelings and slammed doors.

The first key to staying calm is recognizing your emotional triggers. Maybe it's a particular phrase your partner uses, like, "You're overreacting," or the tone they take when they're upset. Knowing what sets you off gives you a chance to prepare for it—or at least recognize when you're about to lose your cool. Once you've identified your triggers, you can work on responding thoughtfully instead of reflexively. Think of it as emotional muscle memory: the more you practice, the stronger your response gets.

Another game-changer? **Pause before speaking.** If you feel your frustration boiling over, take a deep breath (or two) before you say anything. This brief moment of silence does wonders for de-escalating your own emotions and prevents you from blurting out something you'll regret. It also gives your partner the impression that you're really thinking about what they're saying—even if, in reality, you're just trying not to scream.

Physical cues can also help you stay grounded. If you notice your shoulders tensing or your jaw clenching, consciously relax those muscles. Sit down if you're pacing, or place your hands palms-down on a table to feel anchored. These small adjustments tell your body, *We're not in danger; we're just having a conversation,* which can help you calm down and stay present.

Another trick is **visualizing the bigger picture.** Arguments often feel more urgent than they really are. Ask yourself, "Will this matter in a week? A year?" Chances are, the answer is no. Shifting your focus to the long-term importance (or lack thereof) of the issue can make it easier to approach the conversation with less intensity. It's amazing how quickly a disagreement about folding towels fades into the background when you remember it's not the hill your relationship needs to die on.

Humor is another underrated calming tool. If the situation isn't too serious, a well-timed joke or playful comment can lighten the mood. For instance, if your partner is ranting about your socks on the floor, you might quip, "I'm just trying to start a museum of modern sock art." Used sparingly, humor can defuse tension and remind you both that you're on the same team. But timing is everything—if your partner is visibly upset, save the jokes for later.

If all else fails, **call for a timeout.** This isn't just for toddlers; it works wonders for adults, too. If you're too overwhelmed to continue the discussion productively, say something like, "I need a few minutes to cool off before we keep talking." The key is to actually come back to the conversation—don't use a timeout as an escape hatch to avoid the issue. Taking a breather gives you both space to calm down and return to the discussion with clearer heads.

It's also worth mentioning that staying calm doesn't mean ignoring your feelings. You can acknowledge your emotions without letting them take control. Saying, "I'm feeling really frustrated right now, and I need a second to gather my thoughts," shows that you're aware of your feelings but not letting them dictate your behavior. Bonus: it keeps your partner from feeling like you're shutting them out entirely.

Staying calm and collected in an argument isn't easy, but it's one of the most powerful ways to keep a disagreement from turning into a disaster. When you approach the conversation with composure, you set the tone for a more constructive dialogue. And once you've mastered staying calm, you can focus on another vital skill: learning the difference between standing your ground and picking your battles wisely.

Fun Examples of "Do's and Don'ts" in Communicating

Communication in arguments is like baking a soufflé: one wrong move, and the whole thing collapses. When emotions run high, even the best intentions can lead to disaster if you don't watch what you're saying. A small tweak in how you phrase things can be the difference between a conversation that solves problems and one that spirals into chaos. And let's face it—chaos is exhausting.

Take absolutes like "always" and "never," for example. Nothing derails an argument faster. If you say, "You never listen to me," your partner's brain immediately starts searching for evidence to the contrary. They'll pull out the mental spreadsheet of every time they *did* listen—like that one time in 2018—and use it to argue why you're wrong. Meanwhile, the actual issue you were trying to address gets buried under a pile of defensiveness. Instead of going nuclear, be specific. If you're upset about them scrolling through their phone during dinner, say, "It bothers me when you're on your phone while we're eating together." Now you've made your point without making them feel attacked.

Another surefire way to torch an argument is dragging up old fights. It's tempting, especially when the current disagreement feels eerily similar to a past one. But saying, "This is just like that time you forgot my birthday!" turns today's issue into a greatest-hits album of every grievance you've ever had. Suddenly, you're arguing about things that happened years ago, and neither of you remembers what started the fight in the first place. Keeping the focus on the present keeps the conversation productive instead of piling on.

Tone also matters—more than we like to admit. A calm, steady voice invites discussion, while sarcasm or exaggerated sighs send the conversation straight into hostility. Telling your partner, "I'm frustrated about how chores are divided," is a lot more constructive than, "Oh, sure, I'll just do everything myself as usual." The first invites a solution; the second all but guarantees eye-rolling and a defensive retort. You may want to make a point, but sarcasm rarely lands the way you hope.

Timing plays a huge role too. Ever tried to address a serious issue five minutes before bed? That's a rookie mistake. No one wants to hash out a disagreement when they're already half-asleep or in the middle of another task. Choosing the right moment—when you're both calm and have the mental bandwidth—sets the stage for success. If you're unsure, a quick, "Is this a good time to talk?" can save you both from unnecessary tension.

Humor, when used carefully, can also work wonders. Imagine your partner is annoyed about how you fold laundry. Instead of diving into a debate about your questionable folding skills, you could say, "I guess my dream of being a professional laundry folder is over." A playful comment like this diffuses tension and shifts the mood. However, timing is everything. If your partner looks like they're ready to launch into a full-blown rant, jokes might be better left for later. Humor should soften the edges, not sharpen them.

Validation is another underused gem in communication. You don't have to agree with everything your partner says to acknowledge their feelings. A simple, "I understand why that upset you," can go a long way. It shows that you're not dismissing their emotions, even if you have your own perspective. And let's be real—sometimes, feeling heard is half the battle.

At the end of the conversation, wrapping things up with kindness makes a world of difference. Even if you haven't resolved everything, saying, "I'm glad we talked about this," helps both of you walk away feeling like you're on the same team. It's a reminder that the goal isn't to win the argument but to build understanding.

Communicating well during an argument takes practice, patience, and the occasional deep breath. But with a little effort, even the trickiest discussions can become opportunities to strengthen your bond. And if you're wondering when to dig in and when to let go, the next chapter will show you how to pick your battles—because not every argument is worth the energy, no matter how tempting it feels in the moment.

SIX

The Art of the Apology - When and How to Say Sorry

Apologizing in a relationship is a bit like assembling IKEA furniture—you know it's important, it's probably going to make things better, but it's also a process that feels unnecessarily complicated. Sure, you could slap together a quick, "Sorry," and hope it holds, but without the proper effort and sincerity, your apology is about as sturdy as a wobbly shelf. One wrong move, and it all comes crashing down.

Apologies are tricky because they're tied up with pride, vulnerability, and, let's face it, the nagging fear that saying sorry means admitting defeat. But here's the twist: in a healthy relationship, apologies aren't about losing or winning. They're about repairing the connection and showing your partner that their feelings matter more than your ego.

In this chapter, we're diving into the fine art of apologizing. You'll learn why "Sorry you feel that way" isn't a real apology, how to deliver a heartfelt mea culpa without sounding like you're reading from a script, and why a good apology often involves more than just words. Apologizing might not be fun, but when done right, it's the relationship equivalent of pressing the reset button—and that's something worth mastering.

Why Apologies Matter and How to Make Them Heartfelt

Apologies are like Band-Aids for relationships: they don't erase the wound, but they help it heal faster. Yet, despite their importance, so many apologies come out wrong. We've all been on the receiving end of a half-baked "Sorry, I guess," or worse, "I'm sorry you feel that way." Instead of soothing the situation, these non-apologies are the emotional equivalent of pouring salt in the wound. They miss the mark, leaving the hurt party feeling even more dismissed.

So, why do apologies matter so much? For starters, they're a way to acknowledge someone else's pain. An apology says, "I see that I hurt you, and I care enough to address it." Without that acknowledgment, conflicts tend to linger, growing like mold in the corners of your relationship. Apologies clear the air and pave the way for reconciliation. They also show humility—a willingness to put love above pride. And let's be honest, humility isn't always easy to muster when you're certain that *technically* you weren't wrong.

But a good apology is more than just saying the word "sorry." It's about intention and delivery. A heartfelt apology includes three key components: acknowledgment, regret, and a willingness to make things right. Think of it as the holy trinity of mea culpas. First, you acknowledge what you did wrong: "I snapped at you earlier, and I know that was hurtful." Next, express genuine regret: "I feel terrible for how I made you feel." Finally, offer a plan to repair the damage: "I'll try to communicate better next time instead of losing my temper."

Notice what's missing? Excuses. The moment your apology turns into "I'm sorry, but..." you've undermined the whole thing. Adding "but" shifts the focus back to defending yourself, and the apology suddenly becomes about *you* instead of the person you hurt. It's like baking a beautiful cake and then smashing it with a spoon before serving it—completely counterproductive.

Sincerity is another crucial ingredient. People can smell a fake apology from a mile away. If you're apologizing just to end the argument, your partner will pick up on it, and the tension will linger. A good apology requires vulnerability. It's not just about saying the right words; it's about truly meaning them.

And don't underestimate the power of timing. Apologizing too soon, before your partner has had a chance to process their feelings, can feel dismissive. Apologizing too late, on the other hand, risks making the issue seem trivial. The sweet spot is when emotions have calmed just enough for the apology to be heard without reigniting the argument. If you're unsure, try starting with, "Can we talk about earlier? I owe you an apology."

Of course, words alone aren't always enough. Sometimes, actions are needed to back up the apology. If you forgot your anniversary, a sincere "I'm sorry" might be more effective when paired with dinner reservations and flowers. It's not about buying forgiveness but showing that you're willing to put effort into repairing the hurt. In some cases, actions speak louder than even the most eloquent apologies.

Humor, when used carefully, can also play a role in an apology. If the situation allows, a lighthearted comment can show humility and diffuse tension. "I'm sorry I acted like a hangry toddler earlier. Next time, I'll grab a snack before we argue." This works best when the issue isn't too serious, and your partner appreciates humor as a coping tool. Just make sure the joke doesn't overshadow the sincerity of the apology.

At its core, an apology is about connection. It's a way of saying, "I value you more than my pride." And while apologizing might not undo the hurt, it shows your partner that you're willing to take responsibility—a vital step in rebuilding trust. Once you've nailed the art of saying sorry, the next challenge is knowing when and how to admit mistakes without feeling like you've lost the upper hand. After all, being wrong isn't a weakness; it's an opportunity to grow.

Steps to Deliver a Sincere Apology That's Well-Received

Delivering a sincere apology is more than just saying the word "sorry" and hoping for the best. It's an art form, a carefully constructed combination of words, tone, and timing. Done right, it can heal wounds and bring you closer to your partner. Done poorly, it can make things worse—like trying to put out a fire with gasoline. So, how do you apologize in a way that doesn't backfire?

First, start with genuine acknowledgment. No one wants an apology that begins with a vague, "If I hurt you, I'm sorry." That "if" undermines the whole thing. Instead, be specific: "I'm sorry I interrupted you during dinner. I realize it made you feel unheard." This shows your partner that you understand what went wrong and why it upset them.

Next, express regret without turning it into a pity party. "I feel terrible about how I handled that," is a solid start. Avoid phrases like, "I guess I'm just the worst, huh?" which make the apology about you instead of the person you hurt. Apologies aren't a time for fishing for reassurance—they're about showing your partner that their feelings matter more than your ego.

Timing is everything. If your partner is still in the middle of venting their frustrations, jumping in with an apology might feel dismissive. On the other hand, waiting too long can make you seem indifferent. A well-timed apology happens when emotions have settled just enough for it to be heard without reigniting the argument. If you're unsure, start with, "I want to apologize, but I want to make sure you're ready to talk first."

Delivery is key. Your tone should match the gravity of the situation. A monotone, "Yeah, sorry," muttered while scrolling on your phone won't cut it. Neither will an overly dramatic, "I'm soooo sorry!" that comes off as insincere. Speak calmly and look your partner in the eye. Your body language should match your words—no crossed arms, no defensive postures. The goal is to show that you're open and genuine.

Humility is also crucial. A good apology isn't about proving you're right or justifying your actions. It's about taking responsibility. Skip the excuses. Saying, "I'm sorry, but I was just so stressed," shifts the blame away from your behavior and onto the circumstances. Even if your stress was a factor, your partner doesn't want to hear excuses— they want to hear that you're owning your mistake.

A true apology also includes a plan to do better. If your partner feels like the same issue keeps happening, they'll be skeptical of your sincerity. Saying, "I'll make an effort to listen more next time," or, "I'll set a reminder so I don't forget again," shows that you're serious about improving. It's not just words—it's a commitment to change.

Sometimes, words alone aren't enough. Actions can reinforce your apology and show your partner that you mean it. If you forgot their birthday, for instance, a heartfelt apology might go further when paired with a thoughtful gesture, like planning a makeup celebration. Actions don't erase mistakes, but they do demonstrate effort, which goes a long way in rebuilding trust.

And let's not forget humor—used sparingly, it can soften the edges of an apology. If you're apologizing for snapping at your partner because you were hangry, a comment like, "Sorry, I turned into a Snickers commercial," can lighten the mood. Just make sure the joke isn't at their expense, and only use humor if the situation isn't too serious.

After delivering your apology, don't rush your partner for forgiveness. "I said I'm sorry; can we move on now?" defeats the purpose. Give them space to process your words. Their timeline for healing might not match yours, and that's okay. An apology isn't about demanding closure—it's about extending an olive branch and letting them decide when they're ready to take it.

Apologies aren't about perfection; they're about sincerity. When delivered thoughtfully, they can turn a moment of conflict into an opportunity for deeper connection. And once you've mastered the art of saying sorry, the next step is creating a plan to prevent the same issues from cropping up again—because growth is what really makes a relationship stronger.

Humor About Admitting Mistakes (Even When You're "Not Wrong")

Admitting you're wrong can feel like trying to swallow a cactus— uncomfortable, prickly, and not something you want to do in public. But relationships aren't about keeping score, and sometimes, even when you're technically *right,* you've got to step up, admit fault, and say sorry. Why? Because nobody wants to hear, "Well, actually, if you think about it..." when they're upset. Trust me, there's no quicker way to turn a small disagreement into a full-blown battle.

Let's be honest: being right is addictive. It's like winning a game you didn't even know you were playing. But being right doesn't necessarily make you the winner in an argument—at least, not in a relationship. Imagine your partner saying, "Okay, fine, you're right. Happy now?" Spoiler: you won't be. Victory tastes a lot less sweet when it's served with sarcasm and resentment.

This is where humor can save you from digging your heels in too deep. Let's say you've spent the last 15 minutes insisting that your way of loading the dishwasher is superior. You could keep arguing, or you could laugh it off with, "You know, maybe I've missed my calling as a dishwasher efficiency consultant." Self-deprecating humor shows your partner you're not taking yourself too seriously and helps defuse the tension. Plus, it makes you more likable—who doesn't love someone who can laugh at themselves?

Of course, admitting fault doesn't mean rolling over and taking all the blame for everything. It's about owning up to your part of the conflict. If you've been a little snippy because you're stressed, say so: "I realize I've been short with you today, and I'm sorry. That wasn't fair." Owning your actions is powerful—it shows your partner that you're self-aware and care about how your behavior affects them.

The trick is to avoid the dreaded *fake* apology. You know the one: "I'm sorry you feel that way." It's not really an apology—it's a sneaky way of saying, "This is your problem, not mine." If you're tempted to say it, stop and reframe. Instead of dismissing their feelings, acknowledge them: "I'm sorry I made you feel that way." See the difference? One validates their emotions; the other invalidates them entirely.

Sometimes, the hardest part is letting go of the need to explain yourself. We've all been there: "I only said that because I was tired!" While it's okay to provide context, over-explaining often comes across as justifying your actions. Your partner doesn't need a dissertation—they need to feel heard. Keep it simple: "I was wrong to snap at you, and I'll work on that." Short, sweet, and surprisingly effective.

If the idea of admitting fault still makes you squirm, consider this: admitting you're wrong doesn't make you weak—it makes you trustworthy. Nobody expects perfection, but they do expect honesty. Owning up to a mistake shows your partner that you're willing to put the relationship above your pride. It's like saying, "We're on the same team, even when I mess up."

Humor can also help when the apology feels awkward. If you're struggling to admit fault, try easing into it with a playful comment. "I guess I might've been a little dramatic when I said the garbage situation was a personal attack on my soul." It acknowledges your mistake while keeping the mood light. Just be sure the humor feels genuine—this isn't the time for sarcasm or minimizing their feelings.

And finally, know when to stop talking. Once you've apologized, let it breathe. Don't rush to fill the silence with, "But you also…" or, "So we're good, right?" A heartfelt apology should stand on its own. Trust that your partner will appreciate the effort, even if it takes them a little time to respond.

Admitting you're wrong isn't about waving a white flag or losing an argument. It's about prioritizing the relationship over your ego. And when both people are willing to own their mistakes, it creates a foundation of trust and mutual respect. Next, we'll explore how to turn apologies into a "repair plan" for your relationship—because saying sorry is just the beginning of making things better.

Tips for Creating a "Repair Plan" Together

Apologizing is a great first step, but saying "sorry" alone doesn't magically fix everything. It's like patching a hole in a boat without addressing why it sprung a leak in the first place. That's where a "repair plan" comes in—a collaborative effort to ensure the same argument doesn't rear its ugly head again next week.

Think of a repair plan as relationship maintenance. It's not about pointing fingers or keeping score. Instead, it's about asking, "How can we both make this better?" After all, if one person is constantly apologizing while the other waits with arms crossed, resentment builds, and the cycle of conflict continues. A solid repair plan requires both partners to roll up their sleeves and work together.

Start by identifying what went wrong. Let's say the argument was about forgetting an important date. After apologizing, ask, "What would have helped in that situation?" Maybe your partner would appreciate a shared calendar or a reminder system. The point isn't to dwell on the mistake—it's to brainstorm practical ways to avoid it in the future.

A repair plan also means being realistic. If your partner's solution is "never mess up again," that's not exactly helpful. Instead, focus on small, achievable changes. If you've been guilty of snapping when stressed, for example, a repair plan might involve agreeing to step away for a few minutes to cool off before continuing the discussion. It's not about perfection—it's about progress.

This process is also a chance to show empathy. When you ask your partner, "What can I do to make this better for you?" you're signaling that their feelings are valid and that you care about their needs. It's not a performance—it's an opportunity to deepen your connection. Just make sure you follow through on what you agree to; empty promises are worse than no plan at all.

Repair plans aren't one-sided. If your partner has areas to improve, address them gently. For instance, "It would really help if you told me how you feel sooner, so things don't build up," is a constructive way to share your perspective without making it sound like a demand. The goal is teamwork, not turning the conversation into a blame game.

Humor can also play a role in creating a repair plan. If the argument was about something silly—like leaving socks in random places—you might say, "Okay, I promise to stop treating the house like a sock scavenger hunt." A little levity shows that you're taking responsibility without making the conversation overly heavy. Of course, save the jokes for lighter topics—if the disagreement was about something serious, keep it thoughtful and sincere.

The timing of a repair plan is important, too. If emotions are still raw, it's better to let things settle before diving into solutions. Rushing into "fix-it" mode right after an argument can feel dismissive, as though you're trying to skip past the apology stage. A simple, "Can we revisit this later and talk about how to handle it differently next time?" gives both of you time to reflect.

And remember, a repair plan isn't set in stone. Life happens, and things might not always go as planned. If something isn't working, revisit the conversation. Maybe that shared calendar you both agreed on isn't being used, or the stress-cooling-off period needs adjustments. The key is to view the plan as a flexible guide, not a rigid rulebook.

Finally, celebrate progress. If you notice positive changes—like your partner making an effort to communicate earlier or you keeping your cool during a tense moment—acknowledge it. "I really appreciated how we handled that conversation yesterday" reinforces the idea that you're growing as a team. Positive reinforcement goes a long way in building new habits.

A repair plan is about more than just solving one issue—it's about creating a stronger foundation for your relationship. When you both feel heard, supported, and invested in making things better, even the toughest arguments become opportunities for growth.

And speaking of growth, the next chapter will explore how to pick your battles wisely—because sometimes, the best way to avoid needing a repair plan is knowing when to let something go.

SEVEN

How to Pick Your Battles Wisely

Every couple has that one argument that starts small and then snowballs into a dramatic showdown no one saw coming. Maybe it was over which way the toilet paper roll should face, or whether the dishwasher really needs to be loaded *that* specifically. By the time you've finished your passionate debate, you're not even sure how you got here—or why you care so much about forks being on the top rack.

The truth is, not every argument needs to be had. Some battles are worth fighting, like discussing boundaries or financial decisions. Others—like whose turn it is to refill the Brita pitcher—might not be worth the emotional energy. The art of picking your battles isn't about avoiding conflict altogether; it's about saving your energy for the issues that actually matter.

In this chapter, we'll explore how to tell the difference between a minor annoyance and a hill worth dying on. You'll learn to spot the arguments that strengthen your relationship versus the ones that just drain your patience. And who knows? You might even discover that sometimes, letting go of the little stuff feels even better than being right.

Recognizing the Difference Between Minor Issues and Real Problems

Not all arguments are created equal. Some are essential for the health of your relationship—like addressing how to split responsibilities or discussing future goals. Others? Well, they're about the thermostat being set to "arctic tundra" or the milk being left on the counter for five minutes. Recognizing which issues truly matter and which ones you can let slide is the secret to saving your sanity and your relationship.

Let's start with the obvious: not every annoyance needs to turn into a full-blown argument. Sure, it's irritating when your partner leaves their socks in the living room or forgets to replace the toilet paper roll, but is it worth the emotional energy of starting a debate? Sometimes, the answer is "no." Constantly nitpicking or turning every small thing into a battle creates unnecessary tension. Over time, this can make your partner feel like they're walking on eggshells—and no one wants to live like that.

So how do you know when to let something go? Ask yourself this simple question: *Will I remember this in a week?* If the answer is no, it's probably not worth your energy. Minor annoyances—like an unwashed dish or a forgotten errand—are often better handled with humor or a lighthearted reminder than a confrontation. For example, instead of saying, "Why can't you ever wash your plate?" try, "I see your plate auditioning for 'Worst Spot in the Sink' again." It gets the point across without turning the kitchen into a battleground.

But what about the bigger issues? Problems that touch on respect, trust, or shared values aren't just annoyances—they're cracks in the foundation of your relationship. If your partner consistently dismisses your feelings or neglects responsibilities you both agreed on, those aren't things to sweep under the rug. Addressing these issues, even if it's uncomfortable, is essential for a healthy partnership.

The trick is to approach these discussions intentionally. Instead of letting frustration build until you explode, bring up the issue calmly and directly. Saying, "Can we talk about how we divide the chores? I'm feeling overwhelmed," is much more productive than angrily muttering, "Of course I'm doing this again." Addressing real problems is about seeking solutions, not scoring points.

Sometimes, what seems like a small issue is actually masking a deeper concern. For instance, you might think you're arguing about leaving wet towels on the bed, but the real problem is feeling like your contributions aren't appreciated. If an argument keeps resurfacing or seems disproportionately emotional, take a step back and ask yourself what's really bothering you. Addressing the underlying issue can prevent future blowups over the same topic.

It's also worth considering your partner's perspective before jumping into a fight. What feels minor to you might be a big deal to them—or vice versa. For example, if they're upset about the way you fold the laundry, it might not just be about the creases. Maybe they see it as a lack of care for something that's important to them. In these moments, empathy is your best tool. Try to understand their point of view before dismissing the issue as trivial.

On the flip side, if you're the one who tends to get caught up in the small stuff, it's helpful to pause and reflect. Ask yourself, *Is this really about my partner, or am I just stressed, tired, or hangry?* Many minor irritations aren't about the actual "offense" but about something else entirely—like a bad day at work or a sleepless night. Recognizing when your mood is fueling the argument can save both of you a lot of grief.

At its heart, picking your battles is about protecting the emotional climate of your relationship. Constantly arguing over small things drains your energy and can make you both feel like adversaries instead of partners. By focusing on the issues that truly matter, you create space for meaningful conversations and solutions.

And once you've mastered the art of choosing your battles, the next step is learning to let go of those small annoyances without harboring resentment. Because even when you decide not to fight, holding onto frustration can be just as damaging as the argument itself.

Exercises to Evaluate Which Arguments Are Worth Having

Picking your battles isn't about avoiding all arguments; it's about learning to choose the ones that matter. But how do you decide when to speak up and when to let it slide? That's where a little self-reflection—and a dash of humor—can come in handy. Think of this as a mental checklist for figuring out whether a disagreement deserves your energy or is best left in the pile of "things to laugh about later."

Step One: The Emotional Thermometer

Before diving into an argument, take your emotional temperature. Are you angry, annoyed, or just in a bad mood? If you're bringing up an issue because you're cranky or hangry, pause. Have a snack, take a breath, or go for a quick walk. You'd be surprised how often the "big issue" you're ready to tackle disappears once you've dealt with your own emotions. After all, no one argues well when their brain is fueled by frustration and empty carbs.

Step Two: The Five-Year Test

Ask yourself: *Will this matter in five years?* Heck, will it matter in five days? If the argument is about something trivial—like whose turn it is to refill the soap dispenser—it might not be worth the energy. Save your emotional bandwidth for issues with long-term significance, like shared goals, financial decisions, or respecting boundaries. Trust me, you'll thank yourself later.

Step Three: The Balance Sheet of Annoyance

Think of your relationship like an emotional bank account. Every disagreement makes a withdrawal, while positive interactions make deposits. If you're constantly "withdrawing" over minor annoyances, you risk running into the red. Instead of spending emotional currency on whether the toothpaste cap gets screwed back on, save it for moments when a conversation truly needs to happen.

Step Four: The Third-Person Test

Imagine explaining the argument to a friend—or better yet, to someone who doesn't know you at all. If it sounds ridiculous out loud, it's probably not worth the fight. For example, "I can't believe we're arguing because they keep putting the peanut butter in the fridge!" might feel justified in the heat of the moment, but hearing it said aloud often puts things in perspective. (Spoiler: no one else cares where the peanut butter lives.)

Step Five: The "Why" Behind the Fight

Sometimes, small arguments aren't really about the surface issue. If you find yourself repeatedly annoyed by the same thing, dig deeper. Are you frustrated because your partner left their socks on the floor, or because it feels like they're ignoring your efforts to keep the house clean? Addressing the underlying concern—"I feel unappreciated" —is far more productive than spiraling into a debate about footwear.

Step Six: The Let-It-Go Test

If you decide not to argue, ask yourself: *Can I truly let this go?* Choosing not to fight is only helpful if you're genuinely okay with moving on. If you're going to bottle up resentment and revisit it later in a passive-aggressive comment, it's better to have the conversation now. Letting things slide should feel like a relief, not like swallowing a stone.

Step Seven: The Comedy Factor

Finally, ask yourself: *Can this become a funny story later?* Some arguments are so absurd that they're better off being laughed at than argued over. If your partner keeps leaving half-empty cups of water all over the house, try joking about it: "Are we starting a water museum?" Humor not only defuses tension but also reminds you both that life—and love—doesn't have to be so serious all the time.

Learning to evaluate arguments doesn't mean avoiding conflict entirely—it means being intentional about what you address and how. When you save your energy for the battles that truly matter, you'll find that your relationship feels lighter, more focused, and less bogged down by petty frustrations.

Of course, even the most minor annoyances can leave a trace of irritation. In the next section, we'll explore how to let go of the small stuff without letting resentment build, so you can focus on what really matters.

Tips for Letting Go of Trivial Things Without Resentment

Letting go of minor irritations in a relationship is easier said than done. Sure, you'd love to brush off the fact that your partner consistently leaves their socks on the floor or forgets to replace the toilet paper roll, but somehow, those small frustrations seem to multiply until they feel like giant neon signs of disrespect. The challenge is learning to let these things go without secretly harboring resentment—or worse, stockpiling them for a future blowout.

The first step in letting go is deciding if the issue is worth your energy. A great litmus test is asking yourself, *Will this still bother me in a week?* If the answer is no, it's probably safe to drop it. Does it really matter, in the grand scheme of things, that they didn't load the dishwasher "the right way"? Probably not. The trick is training your brain to differentiate between momentary annoyances and genuine relationship issues. It's a lot like sorting laundry—you need to separate the delicates from the heavy-duty items.

Humor is your best friend when dealing with trivial annoyances. Let's say your partner keeps leaving their shoes in the middle of the hallway. Instead of launching into a tirade, you might quip, "Ah, the shoes are migrating to their natural habitat again." A lighthearted remark can defuse tension, gently call out the behavior, and maybe even make them laugh. Just make sure your tone is playful, not sarcastic—this is humor, not passive-aggression disguised as a joke.

Another trick? Perspective. Ask yourself why the issue is bothering you so much. Often, small annoyances reflect deeper concerns, like feeling underappreciated or overwhelmed. If the coffee mug left on the counter feels like a personal slight, it might be worth examining whether you're carrying more emotional or physical labor than feels fair. Addressing the larger issue will make the smaller ones feel less significant.

Sometimes, letting go is simply a matter of reframing. Instead of seeing your partner's forgotten laundry as thoughtlessness, try viewing it as a sign of their humanity. Everyone has their quirks, and while they might not notice the mess, they probably don't care when you leave your half-empty water bottles all over the house. This mutual grace can make it easier to let small things slide.

It's also important to check in with yourself. Are you genuinely annoyed with your partner, or is something else fueling your frustration? If you're tired, stressed, or hungry, even the smallest annoyance can feel monumental. Before you bring up an issue, take a moment to ask yourself if you're in the right headspace. A snack, a nap, or a quick break might be all you need to reset.

If you've decided to let something go, commit to truly letting it go. Choosing not to address a small issue is only helpful if you're not silently stewing about it later. Bottling up your feelings can lead to a blowout over something trivial, like the way they squeeze the toothpaste. If you feel like you can't truly move past it, it's better to bring it up calmly rather than let resentment fester.

When you do need to address something, timing and delivery matter. Don't bring up the unwashed dishes when you're already annoyed about something else, or when your partner's rushing out the door. Instead, pick a calm moment and focus on collaboration. Saying, "It would really help if we could keep the sink clear," is much more productive than shouting, "Why do I always have to clean up after you?"

Letting go of the little things doesn't mean you're ignoring your needs. It means you're prioritizing peace and connection over the fleeting satisfaction of pointing out every flaw. By choosing your battles and allowing minor annoyances to roll off your back, you'll save your energy for the moments that truly matter.

And if you're ready for a laugh, the next section tackles the humor in classic argument behaviors—because sometimes, the best way to let go is to laugh it off.

Humor About Arguments That Don't Actually Matter

Some arguments in relationships are necessary—like discussing boundaries or how to handle finances. But others? They're so absurd that you might find yourself mid-fight thinking, *Why are we even arguing about this?* These are the kinds of spats that don't actually matter but somehow escalate into debates worthy of a courtroom drama.

Take the age-old argument about the thermostat. One of you thinks "comfortable" means an icy 65 degrees, while the other is bundled up in three blankets, grumbling about frostbite. Neither of you is wrong (technically), but the battle rages on. It's less about the actual temperature and more about the principle of it—though what that principle is, no one can quite explain.

Then there's the classic *laundry war.* Maybe you like folding towels in thirds, but your partner insists on halves. Does it matter? Probably not. Will you argue about it? Definitely. You might even feel compelled to stage a folding demonstration to prove your way is objectively better. Spoiler alert: it's not. And neither is theirs. But that won't stop you from bringing it up the next time someone complains about chores.

Food disagreements are another goldmine for ridiculous fights. Whether it's about where to order takeout, who ate the last slice of pizza, or whether pineapple belongs on pizza at all, these debates can get oddly heated. One minute you're debating pizza toppings, and the next, you're shouting, "You never listen to me!" as if their stance on pineapple somehow symbolizes their overall lack of care.

Of course, not all petty arguments are about tangible things. Sometimes, they're about memory. "You said we'd leave at six!" "No, I said we'd *be* there by six!" Cue the back-and-forth, each of you more determined to prove you're right than to actually leave on time. It's the kind of argument you'll laugh about later—if you ever make it to the event.

But why do these silly arguments happen in the first place? Sometimes, it's just about proximity. When you spend a lot of time with someone, even the smallest quirks can feel magnified. Other times, it's a way of deflecting bigger emotions. Instead of addressing something serious, you channel your frustration into an argument about how your partner loads the dishwasher. (Yes, the forks go up—but is it worth the fight?)

The beauty of these arguments, though, is that they often remind you how much you care. If you're bickering over whether socks belong in the hamper or on the floor, it's not really about the socks. It's about navigating life together—messy habits and all. That doesn't make it any less irritating when you trip over their shoes for the hundredth time, but it does add a layer of humor to the situation.

So how do you handle these low-stakes battles without letting them spiral? First, embrace the humor. If you catch yourselves fighting about whose turn it is to refill the Brita, pause and say, "This is the dumbest thing we've ever argued about." Nine times out of ten, you'll both start laughing—and maybe even forget why it mattered in the first place.

Perspective helps, too. Ask yourself, *Will I care about this tomorrow?* If the answer is no, it's a sign to let it go—or at least not take it too seriously. You might still feel the urge to point out that you're *technically* right, but is it worth the awkward silence afterward? Probably not.

And sometimes, the best strategy is to just concede. Let them fold the towels their way. Agree to the "wrong" pizza toppings this time. Set the thermostat somewhere in the middle. These small concessions show your partner that the relationship matters more than winning the argument. Plus, you'll save yourself the headache of dragging the fight out longer than the issue deserves.

Ridiculous arguments are inevitable in any relationship, but they don't have to be destructive. By finding the humor in them and keeping your perspective, you can turn even the silliest fights into moments of connection. And speaking of finding connection, the next chapter dives into the art of compromise—because sometimes the best solution is meeting in the middle.

EIGHT

Compromise Without Feeling Like You've Lost

Compromise is a word that sounds noble in theory but often feels like losing in practice. After all, agreeing to meet in the middle can sting when the middle isn't where you wanted to be. It's like wanting pizza, your partner wanting sushi, and somehow ending up eating salad—a choice no one really wanted but both reluctantly agreed on. How is that fair?

In relationships, compromise is less about splitting everything 50/50 and more about finding solutions that leave both of you feeling heard. It's not a contest to see who sacrifices the most; it's about creating a win-win scenario, even if the "win" looks like agreeing to your partner's favorite restaurant this time in exchange for a movie of your choice later.

This chapter is about reframing compromise as a creative tool for connection. We'll explore how to avoid feeling like you've lost, why small concessions can make a big difference, and how to see compromise as an opportunity to build trust and mutual respect. Because when done right, compromise isn't about giving up—it's about growing together.

Strategies for Finding Middle Ground That Works for Both of You

Compromise in relationships often feels like walking a tightrope. On one side, you don't want to feel like you've given too much; on the other, you don't want your partner to feel like they're the one always bending. But true compromise isn't about losing—it's about finding a middle ground where both of you feel heard, respected, and maybe even a little victorious.

The first step is identifying what actually matters. Not every disagreement needs a drawn-out negotiation. Some issues, like family traditions or core values, are worth a deeper discussion. Others—like which takeout to order—might not be worth the emotional energy. Take a moment to ask yourself, *Is this something I really care about, or can I let it go?* Saving your energy for meaningful conversations makes compromise feel more balanced and less like a constant tug-of-war.

Once you've decided the issue is worth addressing, shift your mindset. Instead of thinking, *What do I have to give up?* try asking, *What can we create together?* This small mental adjustment transforms compromise from a battle into a collaboration. Instead of just dividing the pie, you're baking a new one—bigger and more satisfying for both of you.

Take a common scenario: you want to spend Saturday binge-watching your favorite show, but your partner wants to go hiking. Instead of flipping a coin or letting one person "win," try combining the plans. Start with a morning hike and reward yourselves with an afternoon of couch time. Neither person gets everything, but both get something—and the day feels shared rather than divided.

Communication is critical in finding middle ground. If you're both digging your heels in, nothing will budge. Ask open-ended questions like, "Why is this important to you?" or, "What's a fair way to handle this?" Showing genuine curiosity about your partner's perspective not only fosters understanding but also helps you both get creative about solutions. Plus, it softens the tension when the discussion feels stuck.

Flexibility is just as important as communication. Sometimes, one person will give more, and other times, the other will step up. The key is not keeping score. Relationships aren't a competition where you track who sacrificed the most. If you focus on balancing every single compromise, you'll end up frustrated and exhausted. Instead, trust that compromises tend to even out over time. One day, you're giving in on where to eat dinner; the next, your partner is watching your favorite guilty-pleasure TV show without complaining.

Humor can also ease the process of compromise. If you find yourselves stuck over something trivial, like which side of the bed to sleep on during a trip, turn it into a playful challenge. "Alright, rock-paper-scissors, best of three. Winner gets their way!" A little levity turns a potential standoff into an opportunity to laugh together, which often makes the compromise feel less heavy.

Of course, compromise doesn't mean abandoning your needs. If you constantly feel like you're the one conceding, speak up. Saying, "This is really important to me," lets your partner know that this particular issue matters more than most. Healthy compromise isn't about one person always folding—it's about mutual respect. Likewise, be willing to listen when your partner expresses that something is important to them.

Lastly, celebrate your compromises. It might feel silly at first, but acknowledging the effort you both put into finding a solution builds goodwill. Saying, "I appreciate you meeting me halfway on this," reinforces the idea that compromise is about teamwork, not sacrifice. When both people feel seen and appreciated, compromise becomes less of a chore and more of a shared achievement.

Finding middle ground takes patience and practice, but it's one of the best ways to create a partnership that feels equitable and connected. And once you've mastered the art of compromise, you'll discover that even the smallest concessions can lead to big improvements in your relationship.

Next, we'll explore how to reframe compromise itself—seeing it not as a loss but as a shared victory that strengthens your bond.

Recognizing the Importance of Small Concessions

Compromise doesn't always mean grand gestures or splitting everything down the middle. Sometimes, it's the small concessions—the everyday give-and-take—that hold a relationship together. These tiny moments of "okay, we'll do it your way this time" can seem insignificant on their own but add up to a dynamic where both partners feel respected and valued.

Small concessions start with noticing what matters most to your partner. Let's say they have a strong preference for how the dishwasher is loaded. Sure, it might seem trivial to you, but if it's important to them, does it really hurt to adjust your technique? Taking the extra few seconds to align the plates their way isn't just about the dishes—it's about showing that their preferences matter to you.

Of course, small concessions don't mean being a doormat. They're about making mindful choices to keep the peace without sacrificing your own needs. Think of it as a bank account: every time you willingly let them choose the movie or agree to their preferred pizza toppings, you're making a deposit into the relationship. These small acts build goodwill that makes it easier to handle the bigger compromises when they arise.

Humor can be a game-changer when making small concessions. Let's say your partner always wants to stop for coffee on road trips, even when you're running behind schedule. Instead of rolling your eyes, lean into the moment: "Alright, but this coffee better taste like liquid gold." Turning the annoyance into a playful exchange transforms what could have been a minor frustration into a shared laugh.

It's also important to recognize when your partner makes small concessions for you. Did they agree to go to your favorite restaurant even though they were craving something else? Or let you take the "good" side of the bed without comment? Acknowledging these moments with a simple "Thanks for being flexible" goes a long way. It reinforces that you see and appreciate their effort, making them more likely to continue meeting you halfway.

One of the trickiest parts of small concessions is balancing the invisible scale of who gives in more. It's easy to feel like you're doing all the compromising if you're only focused on your efforts. But relationships rarely work in perfect symmetry. Sometimes you'll bend more, and other times your partner will. Trusting that the balance will shift back over time prevents resentment from building.

Perspective is also essential. If you find yourself frustrated by small sacrifices, try reframing them as opportunities to invest in the relationship. For instance, agreeing to go to their friend's gathering might not be your idea of fun, but the time you spend together strengthens your bond. Thinking of concessions as contributions rather than losses makes them feel more rewarding.

If something starts to feel like a recurring sore spot, don't let it fester. Small concessions should be manageable, not one-sided. If you're constantly giving in on the same issue—whether it's housework, social plans, or how you spend your weekends—it's worth having a conversation. Saying, "I've noticed I've been handling X a lot lately; can we work on evening things out?" can reset the balance before it becomes a bigger problem.

Ultimately, small concessions are about showing your partner that their happiness matters to you. They might not remember every little thing you've done to make their life easier, but the overall effect is a relationship where both people feel valued and supported. Over time, these micro-compromises become the glue that keeps your connection strong, even during the rough patches.

And while small concessions are essential, the real magic happens when you reframe compromise itself—not as a loss but as a win-win. In the next section, we'll explore how to see compromise as a creative solution that benefits both partners, rather than a sacrifice that leaves one person feeling shortchanged.

How to Reframe Compromise as a Win-Win Situation

Compromise often gets a bad reputation, mainly because it's so easy to see it as giving up or losing something. But what if compromise could feel like a win for both of you? Instead of focusing on what you're sacrificing, reframing compromise as a creative collaboration can transform how you approach disagreements and make your relationship stronger.

The first step is letting go of the idea that compromise means settling for less. Instead, think of it as building something together. Imagine you and your partner are trying to decide how to spend a weekend. You want to binge-watch your favorite show, and they want to explore a new hiking trail. Rather than arguing over whose plan wins, focus on combining elements of both ideas. Maybe you start the day with a short hike and then reward yourselves with a cozy movie marathon. Neither person gets their original vision, but the result is something you've created together—an experience you'll both enjoy.

This mindset shift is easier when you understand that compromise isn't about keeping score. If you're mentally tallying who's given up more in the relationship, you're setting yourself up for resentment.

Healthy compromise isn't transactional—it's rooted in trust. Sometimes, you'll give a little more; other times, your partner will. Over time, it balances out, but only if you're focused on the bigger picture rather than the immediate trade-off.

Communication is key to reframing compromise as a win-win. Instead of approaching the discussion as a debate, treat it like a brainstorming session. Use phrases like, "What can we do that works for both of us?" or, "How can we make this feel fair?" These questions encourage collaboration rather than competition, making it easier to find a solution that satisfies you both.

Let's take a more serious example, like deciding how to handle holiday plans. Maybe you want to spend time with your family, and your partner wants to stay home and relax. Instead of digging in your heels, explore options together. Could you split the holidays between families? Host a small celebration at your place? Agree to alternate years? By focusing on flexibility, you're more likely to find a compromise that feels balanced rather than begrudging.

Humor can also play a big role in reshaping compromise. Imagine you're arguing over what color to paint the living room. You want blue; they want green. Instead of turning it into a standoff, inject a little levity: "How about we go with neither and just let the walls stay beige forever?" Humor softens the tension and opens the door to creative solutions—maybe a mix of both colors or a completely new idea you both love.

Another helpful tactic is focusing on the shared goal behind the compromise. If you're debating how to budget for a vacation, remember that the ultimate goal is to create a meaningful experience together. Shifting the focus from "my way versus your way" to "how do we achieve this together" makes the compromise feel more rewarding and less like a sacrifice.

Celebrating successful compromises can also shift how you view them. When you've navigated a disagreement and found a solution, take a moment to acknowledge it. Saying, "I think we handled that really well," reinforces that compromise is a skill you're both working on—and succeeding at. Over time, this positivity creates a stronger foundation for future negotiations.

Finally, don't forget the importance of gratitude. If your partner makes a concession, let them know you appreciate it. A simple, "Thanks for being flexible," can make all the difference in turning a compromise into a moment of connection. When both people feel valued, the process of compromise becomes less about loss and more about building something stronger together.

Reframing compromise as a win-win isn't about pretending you're always thrilled with the outcome. It's about shifting your focus to what you've gained—a stronger relationship, a deeper understanding of each other, and a sense of teamwork.

Lighthearted Examples of "Creative Compromises"

Compromise doesn't always have to feel like a tug-of-war or a solemn negotiation. Sometimes, the best compromises are the ones that make you laugh—where you both get something you want but in a way that's delightfully unexpected. Creativity turns compromise from something begrudging into something memorable and fun, adding a little levity to what could otherwise be a tense situation.

Take the classic argument over what to watch on TV. One of you wants an action-packed thriller, and the other is in the mood for a rom-com. Instead of going to battle over who gets to hold the remote, why not mix it up? Create your own "Romantic Thriller" movie night—start with their pick, then follow it up with yours. Bonus points if you both play movie critics afterward, debating whether the lead in the rom-com would have survived the car chase from the thriller.

Food is another goldmine for creative compromises. Let's say you want pizza, but your partner is craving sushi. Instead of arguing, meet in the middle—literally. Ever tried a sushi pizza? They exist, and they're a surprisingly perfect blend of both worlds. Alternatively, you could order from both places and stage a mini "food festival" at home. Sure, it's unconventional, but it turns what could have been a conflict into a quirky shared experience.

Then there's the eternal thermostat debate. One of you is always cold; the other lives in a perpetual sauna. Instead of fighting over the number on the dial, get creative. Invest in a heated blanket for the chilly one and a fan for the overheated one. Or, embrace the absurdity of it: designate one room as "Arctic Zone" and another as "Tropical Paradise," and retreat to your climate of choice as needed. Who says you can't turn your home into a multi-climate resort?

Household chores are another area ripe for creative compromise. If you're tired of debating who does what, try gamifying the process. Create a "chore roulette" wheel or a weekly draft where you each pick tasks like it's fantasy football. Adding a sense of fun makes the tasks less daunting, and it's hard to argue about vacuuming when you just won it with a spin of the wheel.

Holidays can also be a challenge, especially when you're deciding how to split time between families. Instead of choosing one over the other, why not host a joint gathering? Sure, it's a little chaotic, but watching your parents try to explain their version of "the right way to carve a turkey" to your partner's parents might just become the stuff of family legends. If combining families isn't an option, alternate years but add a twist—each year, the host family has to include a tradition from the other's playbook. Swedish meatballs at Christmas? Why not!

Even something as mundane as redecorating can be an opportunity for creative compromise. Say you want sleek, modern furniture, but your partner loves vintage charm. Instead of arguing, create a "modern vintage" look. Mix their antique lamp with your minimalist desk. Not only do you end up with a unique style, but you also get to tell the story of how you merged your tastes whenever someone asks, "How did you come up with this?"

One of the best examples of a creative compromise is the "switch-off" method. Let's say you can't agree on a weekend activity. One week, it's your partner's pick, no questions asked. The next week, it's yours. The key to making this work? Fully committing to the other person's plan, even if it's not your favorite. Nothing says love like gamely joining them at a flea market when you'd rather be at home, knowing they'll happily cheer you on at karaoke night next weekend.

At its heart, creative compromise is about shifting the focus from what you're giving up to what you're gaining—shared memories, laughter, and a stronger bond. When you approach disagreements with curiosity and playfulness, even the most stubborn stalemates can turn into moments of connection.

And speaking of connection, the next chapter explores how to reconnect after arguments—because no matter how great your compromises are, every relationship can benefit from a little extra TLC after the dust settles.

NINE

Reconnecting After an Argument

Arguments are inevitable in any relationship, but what happens after the dust settles is just as important—if not more so—than the fight itself. Reconnecting after an argument can feel a bit like approaching a skittish cat: you want to reach out, but you're not sure if you'll get purrs or claws in response. Yet, this is the moment when you have the opportunity to repair, rebuild, and remind each other why you're in this together.

Reconnecting doesn't have to be awkward or complicated. In fact, it can be an opportunity to strengthen your bond and show your partner that your love is bigger than any disagreement. This chapter is all about how to bridge the gap post-argument, using humor, routines, and small gestures to wipe away lingering tension. We'll explore simple, fun ways to say, "Let's move on," that don't involve forced apologies or awkward silences.

Because when it comes to love, the real victory isn't in avoiding arguments—it's in finding your way back to each other every time. Let's get started!

Techniques for Repairing and Reconnecting with Each Other

After an argument, it's natural to feel a bit of emotional whiplash. One moment you're passionately defending your stance, and the next, you're left wondering how to bridge the gap between you and your partner. The good news is that repairing and reconnecting doesn't have to feel like walking on eggshells. With a few thoughtful techniques, you can turn post-argument awkwardness into a chance to grow closer.

The first step to repairing is acknowledging the argument without letting it linger. Avoid the temptation to sweep things under the rug. Saying something as simple as, "I know that got heated earlier, and I'd like to talk about how we can move forward," can work wonders. It shows that you're committed to resolving things and sets a collaborative tone for the conversation.

Timing is everything. Jumping into a "let's fix this" mode too quickly can make your partner feel rushed, especially if emotions are still running high. Give each other some breathing room to process what happened. This doesn't mean giving the silent treatment—it means creating space for reflection. A short break to cool off can turn a tense standoff into a productive discussion.

Active listening is crucial during the repair phase. When your partner is expressing their feelings, focus on truly hearing them without jumping in to defend yourself. Resist the urge to mentally draft your response while they're speaking—this isn't a courtroom, and you're not building a closing argument. Instead, try paraphrasing what they've said to confirm you understand: "So, it sounds like you felt unheard earlier when I interrupted." This kind of acknowledgment fosters connection and shows that you value their perspective.

Another effective tool is apologizing with sincerity. Even if the argument wasn't entirely your fault, taking responsibility for your part in it can pave the way for healing. A heartfelt, "I'm sorry for snapping at you—I was frustrated, but I shouldn't have taken it out on you," goes a long way in easing tension. Pairing the apology with a plan to avoid repeating the behavior ("Next time, I'll take a minute to cool off before we talk") shows that you're invested in making things better.

Physical gestures can also help break the ice. A hug, a squeeze of the hand, or even a playful nudge can signal to your partner that you're ready to reconnect. Sometimes, actions speak louder than words—especially when the words are still hard to find.

Humor is another powerful tool for repairing after an argument. If the fight wasn't too serious, a lighthearted comment can ease tension. For example, if you argued about something silly, like the proper way to load the dishwasher, you might say, "So, do you think the dishwasher will ever forgive us?" Humor, when used with care, reminds both of you that even disagreements don't have to feel like the end of the world.

Lastly, remember that reconnecting is a process, not a single moment. Some arguments are resolved quickly, while others take time to fully unpack. What matters most is your willingness to engage with each other and prioritize the relationship over the need to "win." By showing empathy, taking responsibility, and finding ways to bridge the gap, you're building a foundation of trust and resilience that will carry you through future conflicts.

Reconnecting after an argument isn't about erasing the disagreement —it's about showing your partner that the relationship matters more than the fight. And once you've mastered these techniques, you'll see that even the most challenging arguments can become opportunities to strengthen your bond.

Next, we'll explore how humor can help you heal and move forward —because laughter really is the best medicine, especially when it comes to love.

How to Use Humor as a Way to Heal and Move Forward

Humor is like a relationship superpower—it can break tension, ease awkwardness, and remind both of you that even the messiest arguments don't have to overshadow the love you share. When used well, a well-timed laugh can turn a sour moment into something you can both smile about later. Of course, humor can be a double-edged sword, so wield it carefully. There's a fine line between defusing tension and accidentally reigniting the argument.

After a fight, humor can act as a gentle "reset button." Let's say you've just had a heated debate over something trivial, like whether a dish should soak overnight or go straight into the dishwasher. Instead of stewing in the silence, you might say, "I've been thinking, and you're right—our sink deserves to be the third roommate." A light comment like this breaks the ice without dismissing the disagreement. It's not about undermining the seriousness of the argument; it's about showing you're ready to move forward.

One of the best times to use humor is when the argument was over something absurd. If you argued about who forgot to close the cereal box, you could jokingly propose a "cereal treaty" where both parties sign a contract pledging to ensure the box is always sealed. Turning a ridiculous argument into something playful acknowledges its silliness and makes it easier to let go.

Another way humor helps heal is by creating shared inside jokes. These little moments of levity become part of your relationship's unique language. If you once had an argument about the best way to fold towels, you might jokingly refer to yourself as the "Towel Czar" whenever laundry comes up. Inside jokes take the sting out of past conflicts and reinforce the idea that you're in this together, even when you don't see eye to eye.

But tread carefully—humor should always be kind. If your partner is still visibly upset, a joke about the fight might come across as dismissive or even cruel. Timing is everything. Pay attention to their mood and body language. If they're not ready to laugh, save the joke for later and stick to more straightforward ways of reconnecting, like apologizing or listening.

Self-deprecating humor is often a safe bet. Admitting your own flaws with a smile can show your partner you're not taking yourself too seriously. For example, if you realize you've been stubborn during an argument, you might say, "I guess my inner debate champion got carried away again." This kind of humor shows humility and invites your partner to see the lighter side of the situation without putting the blame on them.

Using humor to move forward isn't about ignoring the issue—it's about creating space for resolution. Sometimes, a well-placed joke can even make the apology process smoother. If you forgot your partner's coffee order and it sparked a mini-fight, you might say, "I'd like to formally apologize to the Court of Caffeine for my gross negligence." It softens the moment, making it easier to transition into a genuine apology.

Of course, humor isn't the solution for every argument. Serious conflicts—those involving deep emotions, trust issues, or sensitive topics—require a more thoughtful approach. In these cases, humor might feel out of place or disrespectful. But for lighter disagreements or moments of post-argument awkwardness, humor is a powerful way to say, "Hey, we're still okay."

Over time, using humor to heal becomes second nature. It reminds you both that no argument is bigger than your connection and that even in conflict, you can still find reasons to smile. And while laughter won't fix everything, it can help you take that first step toward moving on.

Speaking of moving on, next we'll dive into creating routines that prevent lingering tensions—because while humor helps, consistency and habits are what truly keep arguments from hanging around too long.

Creating Routines to Prevent Lingering Tensions

After an argument, it's tempting to assume everything is resolved just because you've apologized or shared a laugh. But without a plan to keep things from bubbling up again, tensions can linger like an unwelcome guest. That's where routines come in. By establishing habits that promote emotional recovery and prevent resentment, you create a relationship environment where arguments don't stick around longer than they should.

One simple but effective routine is a **"post-argument check-in."** This isn't about rehashing the fight but ensuring that both of you feel truly heard and ready to move on. For instance, the day after an argument, you might say, "I just wanted to make sure we're okay after yesterday. Is there anything else you want to talk about?" This small gesture shows you care about your partner's feelings and helps prevent unresolved issues from festering.

Another great habit is having **a go-to ritual for resetting your connection.** Maybe it's sharing a hug, taking a walk together, or watching an episode of your favorite sitcom. These rituals signal to both of you that the fight is over and it's time to reconnect. For example, if you've had a disagreement about something mundane, like laundry, you might agree to grab ice cream after the chores are done. It's a small but symbolic way of saying, "We're back on the same team."

For couples who find themselves stuck in recurring arguments, **weekly "state of the union" talks** can work wonders. Set aside time to discuss how things are going—what's working, what's not, and what could be improved. These conversations are less about addressing specific fights and more about maintaining open communication. When you regularly address small issues, they're less likely to blow up into major conflicts.

Creating routines for emotional regulation can also prevent arguments from spiraling. If you know that one or both of you tends to react impulsively in the heat of the moment, agree on a "cooling-off" period during arguments. This might look like stepping away for 10 minutes to collect your thoughts before continuing the discussion. Over time, this habit trains both of you to handle disagreements with more patience and clarity.

Humor can even be part of your post-argument routine. If the argument wasn't too serious, establish a lighthearted tradition for moving on. For instance, you might send each other a funny meme after a disagreement or invent a silly code word like "pineapple" to signal when you're ready to let it go. These quirky routines make arguments feel less daunting and remind you both that your relationship isn't defined by conflict.

Routine acts of kindness also help prevent lingering tensions. If your partner has had a tough day or if you've recently had a disagreement, small gestures—like making their favorite coffee or leaving a thoughtful note—show them you care. These little moments of consideration create an emotional buffer that softens the impact of future conflicts.

Physical routines can be just as effective as emotional ones. Activities like cooking dinner together, going for an evening walk, or having a no-phones hour every night foster connection and reduce stress. When you regularly spend quality time together, arguments lose their staying power because your focus shifts back to shared experiences and mutual appreciation.

Finally, practice gratitude as a daily routine. Take turns acknowledging something you appreciate about each other, whether it's during dinner, before bed, or via a quick text. Gratitude rewires your brain to focus on the positive aspects of your relationship, making it easier to move past conflicts without holding grudges.

Establishing routines for recovery and connection doesn't mean you'll never argue again, but it does mean those arguments will feel less like earthquakes and more like speed bumps. With consistent habits that promote understanding and prevent lingering tension, you'll find it easier to leave disagreements in the past and enjoy the present.

And when it comes to leaving arguments behind, sometimes the trickiest part is finding the right way to say, "Let's move on." In the next section, we'll explore fun and creative ways to do just that—without the awkwardness.

Fun Ways to Say "Let's Move On" Without Awkwardness

After an argument, there's often a moment of hesitation where both of you wonder, *So... are we good now?* It's a delicate dance—neither person wants to push too soon or seem dismissive of the other's feelings. That's where a little creativity and humor can work wonders. Finding lighthearted, fun ways to say, "Let's move on," makes the transition from conflict to connection feel natural, not forced.

One playful approach is using a code phrase. Maybe you decide together that saying, "Truce and tacos?" is your signal that the fight is over and it's time to reconnect. The silliness of a predetermined phrase diffuses lingering tension and provides a shared moment of levity. Plus, who can stay mad when tacos are on the table?

Another option is a simple but symbolic gesture, like a fist bump, a peace sign, or even a goofy high-five. These small physical actions act as a non-verbal way of saying, "I'm ready to move on, if you are." For particularly stubborn fights, you might even go bigger—like offering your partner a "Get Out of Jail Free" card for future disagreements.

It's hard to stay upset when the gesture is lighthearted and a little over-the-top.

If your argument was over something absurd—like the eternal battle of which way the toilet paper roll should face—lean into the ridiculousness. You could stage a "formal debate" where you each give a two-minute speech about your position, complete with props. The act of turning the disagreement into a mock-serious event breaks the ice and ensures you'll both laugh about it later.

Shared rituals are another great way to say, "Let's move on." Maybe you have a go-to playlist that signals it's time to let things go, or you agree to always bake cookies together after a fight. These small, comforting activities help reestablish your bond and create positive associations after moments of conflict.

For tech-savvy couples, sending a funny meme or gif can do the trick. There's something universally disarming about receiving a dancing cat or a "Sorry I was a jerk" e-card in the aftermath of a fight. It's a simple but effective way to show you're ready to reconnect without diving back into the nitty-gritty details of the argument.

If words feel too awkward, physical humor is a solid backup plan. Try "surrendering" by waving a white dish towel or dramatically flopping onto the couch like you've just fought a battle worthy of an epic movie. The exaggerated theatrics help break the tension and remind your partner that you're ready to let the fight go.

And don't underestimate the power of an old-fashioned apology note. Leave a Post-it on the bathroom mirror that says, "I'm sorry for being cranky. Love you!" or slip a handwritten "peace offering" into their book or bag. It's a sweet and unexpected way to say, "We're okay now," without making a big production out of it.

For more stubborn disagreements, plan a "reset" activity together. This could be as simple as taking a walk, playing a board game, or heading out for ice cream. These shared experiences shift the focus from the fight to something fun, giving you both a chance to enjoy each other's company again. Bonus points if you pick something that guarantees laughter, like a comedy show or a karaoke session.

Finally, gratitude can also be a powerful way to move on. Saying, "I appreciate that we were able to talk this through," acknowledges the effort you both put into resolving the argument and reinforces the idea that you're a team. Gratitude closes the door on the conflict and opens the door to connection.

Saying "Let's move on" doesn't have to feel awkward or forced. With a little creativity and a lot of humor, you can transition from conflict to connection in a way that strengthens your bond—and even adds a touch of joy. After all, the goal isn't just to end the argument; it's to remind each other why you're in this together.

And as we look toward the next chapter, we'll dive into managing expectations and expressing needs—because moving forward is even easier when both of you know what to expect.

TEN

Managing Expectations and Communicating Needs

Expectations are the unsung heroes—or villains—of every relationship. Whether they're spoken, unspoken, realistic, or downright ridiculous, expectations have a sneaky way of influencing how we connect with our partners. When managed well, they create harmony and understanding. But when left unchecked, they can lead to resentment, misunderstandings, and the dreaded "I thought you just *knew*" argument.

This chapter is all about taking the guesswork out of managing expectations and expressing your needs. You'll learn how to communicate what's really important to you, understand your partner's boundaries and goals, and avoid the traps of unrealistic assumptions. And because we all carry a few hilariously unspoken expectations, we'll also have a laugh at some of the quirky things we assume about each other without ever saying them out loud.

By keeping expectations in perspective and making communication a priority, you can create a relationship that thrives on clarity, kindness, and a touch of humor. Let's get started!

Expressing Your Needs Clearly to Avoid Unmet Expectations

Communicating your needs might sound simple, but in reality, it's like trying to order food at a drive-thru with a broken speaker: what you say doesn't always match what the other person hears. Yet, clear communication is the foundation of avoiding unmet expectations—and the frustration that comes with them. After all, your partner isn't a mind reader (despite what romantic movies might suggest), so making your needs known is your best shot at getting what you want without resorting to passive-aggressive sighs.

The first step in expressing your needs is knowing what they are. It sounds obvious, but many of us don't take the time to identify what's really bothering us before we bring it up. Instead of saying, "You never help around the house," dig a little deeper. Maybe it's not about the dishes but about feeling overwhelmed or unappreciated. Being clear about the underlying issue makes it easier for your partner to understand—and actually address—your concern.

Once you've identified your needs, how you phrase them matters. Leading with "You always" or "You never" is like throwing gasoline on a tiny flame—it almost guarantees a defensive response. Instead, try using "I" statements to keep the focus on your feelings rather than assigning blame. For example, "I feel stressed when the house is messy, and I'd love if we could figure out a cleaning schedule that works for both of us." It's specific, actionable, and doesn't come across as an attack.

Timing also plays a huge role in clear communication. No one wants to discuss unmet needs during a stressful moment, like right before bed or in the middle of meal prep. Pick a time when both of you are relaxed and more likely to be receptive. A good opening might sound like, "Hey, can we talk about something that's been on my mind?" It sets the tone for a conversation rather than a confrontation.

Humor can also help soften the delivery of your needs. If you're annoyed that your partner keeps forgetting to text you when they're running late, you might say, "I'd love to know you're safe without having to send out a search party!" Playful comments can make potentially touchy subjects feel less heavy, but always gauge your partner's mood before attempting a joke.

It's also crucial to give your partner a chance to respond. Once you've shared your needs, pause and let them share their perspective. A conversation is a two-way street, and listening to their thoughts is just as important as expressing your own. Resist the urge to interrupt or jump in with counterpoints—let them finish, even if you don't agree with everything they say. The goal is understanding, not winning.

A common pitfall in expressing needs is expecting immediate changes. While it's great to communicate your desires, don't forget that your partner is human, too. Adjusting habits takes time, and small steps toward improvement are still progress. For example, if your partner starts cleaning up their shoes but forgets once or twice, acknowledge the effort rather than pointing out the slips.

Lastly, express gratitude when your partner meets your needs. It's easy to assume they "should" just do these things because you've asked, but everyone likes to feel appreciated. Saying, "Thank you for taking care of the dishes last night—it really meant a lot," reinforces positive behavior and encourages them to keep it up.

Clear communication about your needs isn't just about avoiding conflict—it's about fostering a deeper connection. When both of you feel comfortable expressing what's important, it creates an atmosphere of trust and mutual respect.

Of course, expressing your needs is only part of the equation. The next step is understanding your partner's boundaries and goals—because a thriving relationship works best when both people's priorities are on the table.

Understanding Each Other's Boundaries and Goals

Every relationship is a balancing act between individuality and partnership. While you may share a lot with your partner—Netflix passwords, snacks, and maybe even a pet—you're still two separate people with unique boundaries and goals. Understanding and respecting those differences is the secret sauce for a healthy, long-lasting connection.

Boundaries can be tricky to navigate because they're not always obvious. Your partner probably hasn't handed you a neatly typed list of things that make them uncomfortable. Instead, you learn their boundaries over time—often the hard way, like when your innocent joke about their singing voice turned into an hour of awkward silence. The key is to recognize these moments as opportunities to understand them better, not as personal failures.

Start by normalizing conversations about boundaries. It's not just about what bothers them—it's also about what makes them feel secure and respected. A simple question like, "Are there things I do that make you uncomfortable, even if I don't realize it?" opens the door for honest dialogue. And don't be defensive if their answer surprises you; this isn't about blame—it's about building trust.

Similarly, don't hesitate to share your own boundaries. If you need time alone to recharge after a stressful day or prefer not to discuss family drama during dinner, let them know. Saying, "I need some quiet time before I can talk about this," isn't rejecting your partner—it's honoring your own emotional limits. Clear communication about boundaries prevents misunderstandings and shows your partner you respect both of your needs.

Goals are just as important as boundaries when it comes to understanding each other. While you might have shared dreams—like buying a house or traveling together—you also have individual ambitions that deserve space to flourish. Ignoring your partner's goals or expecting them to mirror yours can lead to resentment over time. After all, they didn't sign up to be your clone.

One way to align on goals is to set regular check-ins. These don't have to be formal sit-downs with a spreadsheet (unless you're into that). It can be as simple as asking over coffee, "What's something you're working toward right now?" or "How can I support you with your goals?" These small but meaningful conversations remind both of you that your relationship is a team effort.

Humor can make boundary and goal discussions less intimidating. For instance, if your partner sets a boundary about "no phones during date night," you might joke, "What if I'm Googling how to be an amazing partner?" Lighthearted comments like this show you're listening while keeping the mood relaxed. Similarly, if their goal is to run a marathon and you're not exactly sporty, you might say, "I'll be cheering from the sidelines—right next to the snack table!"

One challenge many couples face is when boundaries and goals don't perfectly align. Maybe you need more alone time than your partner, or their goal of switching careers means a temporary financial strain. These situations require empathy and compromise. Start by acknowledging their perspective: "I know this is important to you, even if it's a little tough for me." Then work together to find a solution that respects both your needs.

It's also important to revisit boundaries and goals periodically. People change, and so do their priorities. What worked for your relationship a year ago might need tweaking now. Checking in ensures that both of you feel supported and understood, even as life evolves.

Finally, celebrate your partner's boundaries and goals. If they stand firm on something that's important to them—like sticking to a budget or prioritizing family time—acknowledge it. Similarly, cheer them on as they work toward personal milestones, whether it's landing a new job, running that marathon, or mastering sourdough bread. Showing genuine enthusiasm reinforces that you're invested in their happiness.

By understanding and respecting each other's boundaries and goals, you create a relationship built on mutual respect and support. And once you master that, it's time to tackle the unspoken expectations we all carry—because not everything can be solved with a checklist or a goal-setting session.

Humor About the Unspoken Expectations We All Carry

Unspoken expectations in relationships are like the fine print in a contract—no one explicitly agreed to them, but somehow, they're there, creating misunderstandings and drama. Everyone has these hidden assumptions, from how laundry should be folded to who's responsible for remembering birthdays. And when those expectations collide? Cue the confusion, followed by the inevitable, "How could you not know that?!"

Take the classic toothpaste debate. One of you assumes that the tube should be squeezed neatly from the bottom, while the other couldn't care less as long as toothpaste comes out. It's not like anyone sat down at the start of the relationship and said, "Just so you know, improper toothpaste squeezing is my personal nightmare." But here you are, staring at a mangled tube and wondering what you've gotten yourself into.

Then there's the silent battle over the thermostat. One partner expects the house to feel like a cozy blanket, while the other prefers the icy tundra. No one ever explicitly said, "By the way, my ideal home temperature is 72 degrees, no exceptions." Yet somehow, these unspoken rules clash every winter (and summer), leaving both of you wrapped in passive-aggressive blankets.

Let's not forget the expectation that your partner will automatically know how you're feeling—because, obviously, your sighs are a universal language, right? The truth is, no one can read minds, no matter how many significant glances or dramatic pauses you throw their way. Expecting your partner to intuitively know you're upset because they didn't notice the garbage overflowing is setting both of you up for failure.

And holidays? Oh, the unspoken expectations really come out to play here. Maybe one partner assumes gifts will be wrapped in beautiful paper with handwritten notes, while the other thinks, *A gift bag with tissue paper is plenty of effort.* These mismatched assumptions can lead to hurt feelings, even though neither of you ever discussed what "gift wrapping etiquette" should entail.

The good news is that these unspoken expectations are often hilarious when you take a step back. Instead of stewing over them, why not call them out with humor? For example, if you're always the one to load the dishwasher, you might jokingly say, "I didn't realize 'dish fairy' was in my job description!" Or if your partner keeps expecting you to remember every single password, you could quip, "Did I miss the memo that I'm the official IT department?"

Addressing unspoken expectations with humor makes it easier to discuss them without turning the conversation into an argument. It also gives you both a chance to acknowledge that, yes, some of these assumptions are a little ridiculous. Nobody's perfect, and poking fun at your quirks can remind you both not to take things too seriously.

Of course, humor alone won't solve everything. It's also important to talk about these expectations openly. If something is consistently bothering you, bring it up—not as an accusation, but as a chance to clarify. "I realized I've been expecting you to notice when the trash is full without me saying anything. Can we figure out a better way to handle it?" turns a potential fight into a collaborative conversation.

You might also discover that some of your own unspoken expectations are... a little over the top. Does it really matter if the towels are folded into perfect thirds instead of halves? Are you clinging to an ideal that's causing unnecessary tension? Sometimes, the best way to deal with an unspoken expectation is to let it go entirely.

At the end of the day, acknowledging and laughing about these quirks is what makes relationships fun and uniquely yours. The unspoken expectations aren't going anywhere—they're part of being human. But when you approach them with humor and honesty, they become less of a stumbling block and more of a shared inside joke.

Next, we'll explore how to keep expectations in perspective, ensuring they don't overshadow the connection you've built with your partner.

Tips for Keeping Expectations in Perspective

Expectations are like houseplants—they can add beauty and life to your relationship, but if you're not careful, they'll either wither from neglect or grow so wildly out of control they take over everything. Managing expectations with perspective is about finding the balance between maintaining healthy standards and giving your partner the room to be human (and maybe forget to water the metaphorical plants once in a while).

The first step to keeping expectations in check is recognizing the difference between what's reasonable and what's wishful thinking. Wanting your partner to call when they're running late? Reasonable. Expecting them to always know what you want for dinner without being told? That's drifting into psychic territory. Ask yourself, *Is this something I'd reasonably expect of myself?* If the answer is no, it's time to adjust.

Perspective also requires acknowledging that your partner is a flawed, wonderful, messy human—just like you. They're going to forget things, make mistakes, and occasionally say the wrong thing. If your expectation is that they'll never disappoint you, you're setting them up for failure. Instead, aim for grace. When they stumble, remind yourself that their intentions are likely good, even if their execution occasionally misses the mark.

One way to keep expectations in perspective is by focusing on effort rather than perfection. Let's say your partner offers to cook dinner but burns the pasta. Instead of dwelling on the crispy spaghetti, appreciate the gesture. "Thank you for making the effort; I'll take it from here" goes a lot further than, "Do you even know how boiling water works?" When you focus on the intention behind the action, it strengthens your connection rather than tearing it down.

Another helpful strategy is to be upfront about your expectations instead of assuming your partner knows them. Misaligned assumptions are the root of many relationship conflicts. For example, if you expect Valentine's Day to involve flowers, a heartfelt card, and a grand romantic gesture, but your partner expects a quiet evening at home, neither of you is likely to feel satisfied. Talking about these expectations ahead of time avoids disappointment—and awkward gift exchanges.

Humor can also help when managing expectations. If you've been quietly expecting your partner to magically notice the laundry piling up, you might say with a grin, "I've been waiting to see if the laundry fairy would show up, but it looks like we'll have to handle it ourselves." Playful comments take the sting out of unmet expectations and create an opening for collaboration.

When expectations go unmet, take a moment to reflect before reacting. Ask yourself, *Is this worth bringing up?* Not every disappointment needs to be addressed. If it's a recurring issue or something that truly affects you, it's worth discussing. But if it's a one-off oversight, consider letting it slide. Nobody's perfect, and sometimes the healthiest response is to focus on the bigger picture.

Reframing is another powerful tool for keeping expectations in perspective. Instead of thinking, *They didn't meet my expectation,* try asking, *Did they show me love or effort in a different way?* For instance, maybe they didn't plan an elaborate anniversary date but spent the evening genuinely connecting with you. Looking for the underlying intent can help you appreciate their efforts, even if they don't align perfectly with your ideal.

Finally, remember that not all expectations have to be set in stone. Life changes, and so do people. Revisiting and adjusting expectations as your relationship evolves ensures that they stay realistic and relevant. What worked when you were newlyweds might not work when you're navigating a busy career or parenting together. Being flexible allows you to grow together instead of growing frustrated.

Managing expectations isn't about lowering your standards—it's about aligning them with reality and appreciating the effort and love behind your partner's actions. By keeping expectations in perspective, you create room for kindness, humor, and understanding.

And as we move into the next chapter, we'll explore how to support each other through disagreements, ensuring that even your toughest moments become opportunities to strengthen your bond.

ELEVEN

Supporting Each Other Through Disagreements

Disagreements in a relationship are like bad weather—you can't avoid them forever, but you can prepare for them. Whether it's a light drizzle of annoyance over who left the milk out or a full-blown hurricane about spending habits, the goal isn't just to survive the storm but to come out of it with your relationship umbrella intact.

The trick? Learning to support each other even when you're upset. Yes, that means showing empathy when all you really want to do is roll your eyes dramatically or retreat into a blanket fort. It's about realizing that the argument isn't a boxing match, where one of you gets to claim victory and a shiny belt. It's more like building IKEA furniture together: frustrating, a little chaotic, but ultimately rewarding if you can figure out which piece goes where.

In this chapter, we'll cover how to balance your individual feelings with the overall health of your relationship, keep mutual respect alive (even when you're seeing red), and master the delicate art of "taking turns" as the peacemaker. Spoiler: no one wants to be the bigger person all the time, but sometimes you've got to grab that moral high ground and hold it—for the team.

By the end, you'll see that disagreements, while not exactly fun, can actually bring you closer if you approach them with a mix of empathy, humor, and maybe a snack for good measure. Let's get started!

How to Show Empathy and Understanding Even When Upset

Showing empathy during an argument can feel like trying to hug a porcupine—it's awkward, uncomfortable, and all you really want to do is protect yourself from those metaphorical quills. But empathy is one of the most powerful tools you have when navigating a disagreement. It's the secret sauce that turns "me versus you" into "us against the problem."

First, let's acknowledge the obvious: it's hard to be empathetic when you're upset. Your brain wants to focus on how *you're* feeling, not what's going on with your partner. But here's the thing—empathy doesn't mean ignoring your own emotions; it means recognizing that both of you are carrying feelings that deserve attention. Think of it as emotional multitasking: you can validate their frustration while still honoring your own.

A great way to start is with active listening. No, this doesn't mean sitting silently while mentally drafting your counterpoints. Real listening involves focusing on what your partner is saying and trying to understand their perspective. For example, if they're upset because you forgot an important date, don't jump straight to defending yourself. Instead, try saying, "I can see why that hurt your feelings, and I'm sorry it felt like I wasn't prioritizing you." That's empathy in action— and it works way better than a defensive, "Well, I've been busy!"

Sometimes, empathy is about looking beyond the words. If your partner is snapping about dishes in the sink, it might not be about the dishes at all. Maybe they're overwhelmed or feeling unappreciated. Asking, "Is something else bothering you?" can open the door to a deeper conversation. (Bonus points if you actually tackle the dishes while you talk.)

Body language matters, too. If you're standing with your arms crossed and a look that says, *Can we just get this over with?* it's not exactly screaming, "I care about how you feel." Instead, try open, relaxed postures that show you're engaged. And if eye contact feels too intense, a small physical gesture—like holding their hand or sitting closer—can convey empathy without saying a word.

Humor can also be a surprising ally. Let's say your partner is venting about something that feels blown out of proportion, like the way you organize the spice rack. Instead of brushing it off, you might say, "Clearly, my laissez-faire paprika placement has offended the spice gods." It's playful, not dismissive, and can lighten the mood enough for a productive conversation to follow.

But what about when *you're* the one feeling upset? It's still possible to practice empathy, even while advocating for yourself. Start by naming your own emotions clearly: "I'm feeling hurt right now because I don't think my efforts were noticed." Then, invite your partner's perspective: "Can we talk about how we're both feeling and figure out what went wrong here?" Framing the conversation this way keeps things collaborative rather than confrontational.

If the argument escalates, empathy might feel out of reach in the heat of the moment. That's okay—it's better to pause than to push forward without understanding. Taking a short break to cool off gives both of you space to regroup. When you return to the conversation, lead with something empathetic like, "I know we both care about this, and I want to understand your side better."

One of the biggest myths about empathy is that it means agreeing with the other person. It doesn't. You can completely disagree with your partner's stance and still validate their feelings. Saying, "I don't see it that way, but I understand why it matters to you," shows respect without sacrificing your own perspective.

The magic of empathy is that it de-escalates tension and brings you closer, even in the middle of a fight. When both of you feel seen and heard, the argument becomes less about winning and more about finding a solution.

And once you've nailed the art of empathy, the next challenge is balancing your individual feelings with the health of the relationship —because even the most empathetic couples need to remember they're on the same team.

Balancing Individual Feelings with Relationship Health

Disagreements in a relationship often feel like a tug-of-war between "What about *me*?" and "What about *us*?" Balancing your individual feelings with the overall health of the relationship can seem tricky, but it's entirely doable—and crucial. After all, you can't have a strong partnership if either of you feels overlooked or unsupported.

The first step is recognizing that *both* perspectives are valid. Yes, yours too. It's easy to get caught up in your own feelings during an argument, but reminding yourself that your partner's emotions are just as real (and probably just as intense) helps you shift from competition mode to collaboration mode. It's not about whose feelings "win"—it's about making space for both of you to be heard.

Start by taking turns sharing your feelings, like an emotional game of "I go, you go." This might sound tedious, but it works wonders for diffusing tension. For example, you might say, "I felt hurt when you brushed off my suggestion earlier." Then, invite your partner to share their side: "What were you feeling when that happened?"

This approach keeps the focus on understanding rather than escalation.

The tricky part is resisting the urge to dismiss your own emotions for the sake of peace. Sure, it's tempting to avoid conflict by saying, "It's fine, I don't care," when you clearly *do* care. But burying your feelings doesn't make them disappear—it just postpones the explosion for another day. Instead, try a middle ground: acknowledge your emotions without letting them dominate the conversation. "I'm upset about this, but I want us to figure it out together" strikes the right balance.

On the flip side, don't fall into the trap of prioritizing your feelings *over* the relationship. Yes, your emotions matter, but so does the overall health of the partnership. If you find yourself digging in your heels just to prove a point, take a step back and ask, *Am I fighting for what's best for us, or just for me?* Sometimes, letting go of a minor grievance is the most loving thing you can do.

Humor can help shift the focus back to the relationship as a whole. If the argument starts feeling like a standoff, try something playful to remind you both of your shared bond. For instance, if you're debating whose turn it is to clean the bathroom, you might say, "Maybe we just hire a referee and make this official." It's hard to stay mad when you're both laughing at the absurdity of the situation.

Another strategy is to frame the conversation around your shared goals. Instead of "I need you to stop being late," try, "How can we make sure we're both on time and less stressed about plans?" This small tweak shifts the focus from individual blame to collective problem-solving.

Balance also involves knowing when to step back and when to lean in. If you notice that your partner seems overwhelmed during the discussion, consider pausing to give them space to process. "I can see this is a lot right now—let's take a break and come back to it later" is a powerful way to show that you're prioritizing the relationship over immediate resolution.

And don't forget to check in with yourself. Balancing feelings isn't just about managing the argument; it's about staying mindful of your own emotional state. If you're feeling particularly heated or defensive, take a moment to breathe and regroup before continuing. A calm you is much better equipped to handle the balance between "me" and "us."

At the end of the day, balancing individual feelings with relationship health isn't about sacrificing yourself or silencing your partner. It's about creating a dynamic where both of you feel supported and valued, even in the middle of a disagreement.

Of course, someone often has to make the first move toward peacemaking. And in the next section, we'll explore the humor and challenge of "taking turns" being the bigger person—because, yes, sometimes you've just got to go first.

Humor About "Taking Turns" in Being the Peacemaker

Being the peacemaker in a relationship is like drawing the short straw —someone's got to do it, but nobody's thrilled about it. And let's face it, no one wants to *always* be the one who says, "Okay, let's calm down and figure this out." Yet, taking turns as the bigger person is a necessary part of keeping the peace—and it's a lot easier (and funnier) when you embrace the humor in it.

First, let's address the obvious: being the peacemaker often feels like a thankless job. You're sitting there, biting your tongue, offering olive branches, while your partner is still mid-rant about who left the garage light on. It's tempting to think, *Why am I always the one defusing the situation?* But before you declare yourself the household saint, remember this: your partner likely feels the same way sometimes. It's just that their turn hasn't rolled around yet.

The key to surviving (and thriving) as a peacemaker is to embrace the absurdity of it. Let's say your partner is worked up about something minor, like the "correct" way to fold towels. Instead of escalating the argument, you might offer a ridiculous compromise: "How about we iron them into origami swans? That way, no one's happy." Humor diffuses the tension and reminds you both that some battles just aren't worth fighting.

Of course, there are moments when humor alone won't cut it, and you need to step up with a genuine effort to smooth things over. This is when the phrase "taking turns" becomes your mantra. If you've been the peacemaker for three consecutive arguments, it's fair to gently point out, "Hey, I think it might be your turn to be the Zen master this time." Framing it as teamwork rather than a chore keeps resentment at bay.

Another tactic? Playfully overdramatize your role as the bigger person. The next time you're diffusing a silly argument, announce, "I shall now ascend to the throne of emotional maturity and offer a truce!" Bonus points if you dramatically mime placing a crown on your head. It's hard to stay mad at someone willing to make themselves look ridiculous for the sake of peace.

But let's not forget the reality: sometimes being the peacemaker is genuinely tough. Maybe you're still nursing your own frustrations, but you know someone has to take the first step. When this happens, remind yourself that peacemaking isn't about "losing." It's about breaking the cycle of tension and creating space for both of you to feel heard. And hey, if it means you get bonus relationship karma, why not?

On the flip side, if you're not usually the one to extend the olive branch, consider how refreshing it might be to take a turn. There's something empowering about saying, "You know what? Let's stop arguing and figure this out." It shows maturity, and—let's be honest—it's also a great way to score a little extra credit in the relationship.

Who doesn't love a partner who says, "Let's fix this" without being prompted?

One humorous way to formalize the idea of taking turns is to create an actual "peacemaker token." It could be a goofy hat, a trinket, or even a random kitchen utensil like a spatula. Whoever holds the token is officially the peacemaker for that argument. When the spatula comes out, you know it's time to put down your grievances and work toward a solution. It's silly, but it adds a lighthearted touch to the process.

Finally, celebrate your wins as a peacemaker. After a particularly successful resolution, you might say, "Well, that's one for the history books—look at us adulting!" Recognizing the effort it takes to resolve conflicts reinforces that peacemaking is a shared responsibility and not a burden to carry alone.

In the end, taking turns being the peacemaker ensures that no one feels like they're always holding the emotional weight of the relationship. And when you approach it with humor and kindness, you'll find that being the bigger person isn't so bad after all—especially when you know your partner will have your back next time.

Speaking of mutual effort, the next section will focus on ways to keep mutual respect at the forefront, ensuring that even during disagreements, your partnership stays strong and balanced.

Ways to Keep Mutual Respect at the Forefront

Disagreements can test the foundation of any relationship, but keeping mutual respect front and center ensures that even the toughest arguments don't leave lasting damage. Respect is the glue that holds everything together—it reminds you that no matter how heated things get, you're still partners, not adversaries.

One of the simplest ways to maintain respect is to avoid making the argument personal. It's tempting to throw out a zinger like, "You always do this!" or, "You're just like your mother!" in the heat of the moment, but those comments hit below the belt. Instead, stick to the issue at hand. It's the difference between saying, "I felt hurt when you interrupted me," and, "You never listen to me because you only care about yourself!" One keeps the discussion constructive; the other is basically tossing a grenade into the room.

Another way to show respect is by giving your partner the benefit of the doubt. Assume that their intentions are good, even if their execution misses the mark. For example, maybe they forgot an anniversary dinner you mentioned weeks ago. Instead of jumping to, "You clearly don't care about me," try, "I know you didn't mean to forget, but it hurt because it was important to me." A little grace goes a long way toward keeping things civil.

Active listening is another hallmark of mutual respect. It's not just about hearing words—it's about showing that you value your partner's perspective. That means putting down your phone, making eye contact, and nodding occasionally so they know you're engaged. Bonus points if you repeat back what they said: "So you're saying it bothers you when I leave my clothes on the floor?" It might sound simple, but showing you understand their point makes them feel heard, even if you don't agree.

Respect also means avoiding the "silent treatment." Sure, it's satisfying to withhold words like they're a rare commodity, but it's not exactly a productive way to handle conflict. Instead of shutting down, try saying, "I need some time to cool off before we continue." It communicates your need for space without making your partner feel like they're being iced out.

Humor, when used thoughtfully, can help maintain respect during an argument. If you're debating over something ridiculous, like whether a sponge belongs on the counter or in the sink, try saying, "Okay, I think we need a sponge summit to resolve this once and for all." Playful comments like this remind you both that your love is bigger than the current disagreement. Just make sure the humor doesn't come across as dismissive—it's about lightening the mood, not trivializing their feelings.

Respect also involves recognizing your partner's boundaries and honoring them, even when it's inconvenient. If they've expressed that they need some time alone after an argument, respect that request instead of pushing for immediate resolution. It might feel frustrating in the moment, but it shows that you value their needs as much as your own.

Another way to keep respect alive is by avoiding the urge to "win" the argument. In relationships, winning isn't about proving your point—it's about finding a solution that works for both of you. Instead of aiming for victory, aim for understanding. This mindset shift turns arguments into opportunities to strengthen your connection rather than chip away at it.

Finally, don't forget to acknowledge and appreciate each other's efforts. If your partner apologizes or takes a step to resolve the argument, say thank you. "I appreciate that you took the time to talk this through with me," might seem small, but it reinforces that their effort matters. Respect grows when both people feel seen and valued.

Keeping mutual respect at the forefront of your disagreements isn't always easy, but it's one of the most important skills you can develop as a couple. When respect is the foundation, even the messiest arguments become manageable—and sometimes even opportunities for growth.

And speaking of growth, the next chapter will explore how to embrace love through imperfection, showing that your relationship's quirks and flaws are what make it truly one of a kind.

TWELVE

Embracing Love Through Imperfection

Every couple has quirks, flaws, and moments of pure chaos—and that's what makes love so beautifully human. Relationships aren't built on perfection; they're built on the messy, unpredictable, and sometimes downright hilarious realities of life together. The truth is, trying to create a perfect partnership is like trying to keep your living room spotless when you have a puppy: good luck with that.

This chapter is all about embracing the imperfections that make your relationship unique. We'll explore how to celebrate your quirks as a couple, turn arguments into opportunities for growth, and laugh at the wonderfully flawed journey you're on together. Because when it comes to love, it's not about having everything figured out—it's about figuring it out *together*. Let's dive into the joy of imperfection.

Celebrating Imperfections as a Couple's Unique Quirks

Every couple has quirks—the little things that make your relationship yours. Maybe you have a running joke about who snores louder, or perhaps you both insist on arguing over the "right" way to stack the dishwasher, even though you both secretly know neither of you is that good at it. These quirks aren't flaws—they're the fingerprints of your relationship, the things that set your love apart from everyone else's.

Take, for example, those weird habits you've picked up over time. Perhaps you've developed a nightly routine of debating which show to watch but always ending up rewatching *The Office.* Or maybe one of you insists on folding towels a certain way while the other stubbornly refuses to follow the system just for the fun of it. What starts as tiny annoyances often becomes part of your shared story— the stuff you'll laugh about years down the line.

Learning to celebrate these quirks instead of trying to fix them is key to embracing imperfection. Sure, it's tempting to roll your eyes when your partner insists on doing something their way, like turning the thermostat into a battle zone. But what if, instead of being annoyed, you leaned into it? Imagine saying, "Oh no, the Great Thermostat Debate of 2023 has begun!" Turning it into a playful moment transforms a potential fight into a shared laugh.

It's also helpful to remember that every couple's imperfections are unique. What works for one pair might not make sense for another, and that's okay. Maybe you and your partner communicate through a mix of sarcasm and memes, while another couple thrives on long heart-to-hearts. There's no one-size-fits-all approach to love—your relationship's quirks are part of what makes it special.

Sometimes, those quirks even become your greatest strengths. The partner who nags you about the laundry? They're probably the same one who keeps the household running like a well-oiled machine. And the one who constantly forgets the grocery list? They're likely the reason you've discovered some of your favorite "accidental" meals. When you start to see the beauty in each other's flaws, those imperfections become endearing rather than irritating.

Celebrating imperfections also means letting go of the idea that your relationship has to look a certain way. Social media and romantic comedies might try to convince you that love should always be glamorous and effortless, but real love is built in the everyday messiness of life. It's in the nights spent arguing over who left the milk out, the mornings when you're too grumpy to talk, and the moments when you accidentally laugh at the wrong time during a serious conversation.

One of the best ways to embrace these quirks is to document them—not with Instagram-perfect photos, but with inside jokes, silly traditions, and shared memories. Create a running list of the "Top 10 Dumbest Arguments We've Had" or start a scrapbook of your weirdest moments as a couple. Looking back on these snapshots of imperfection can remind you of how far you've come and how much fun you've had along the way.

Humor is your best ally in celebrating imperfections. If one of you has a tendency to lose track of time, you might say, "We'll leave for the party once our resident Time Lord is ready." Or if your partner insists on packing 14 sweaters for a weekend trip, you could quip, "Do you think we're moving to Antarctica?" Laughing together about these quirks diffuses tension and creates a sense of camaraderie.

At the heart of celebrating imperfections is gratitude. Instead of focusing on what's "wrong," focus on what's wonderful about your partner and your relationship. Those quirks you sometimes grumble about are part of the package deal—their unique mix of habits, preferences, and personality traits is what makes them *them*. And when you stop to think about it, you wouldn't want them any other way.

Speaking of quirks, even arguments—yes, those dreaded conflicts—can have a silver lining. In the next section, we'll explore how disagreements can actually strengthen your bond, proving that imperfection isn't just lovable—it's essential.

How Arguments Can Actually Strengthen Your Bond

Arguments get a bad rap. Sure, they can be uncomfortable, frustrating, and occasionally loud, but they're also an inevitable part of any relationship. And here's the twist: when handled well, arguments can actually strengthen your bond. They're like emotional workouts—challenging in the moment but ultimately making you stronger.

The first thing to remember is that arguments aren't inherently bad. They show that both of you care enough to engage. If you didn't, you'd probably just nod, smile, and silently plot your escape every time something annoyed you. Disagreements mean you're invested— and that's a good thing. It's not the argument itself that matters; it's how you navigate it.

In fact, arguments often reveal things about each other that might otherwise stay buried. Maybe your partner's frustration over dirty dishes isn't about the dishes at all—it's about feeling overwhelmed or underappreciated. And maybe your insistence on sticking to a budget isn't just about finances but about wanting to feel secure and future-focused. When you dig into the underlying emotions, you uncover opportunities to connect on a deeper level.

Another way arguments can strengthen your bond is by teaching you how to compromise. Every time you navigate a disagreement, you're practicing skills like listening, empathy, and creative problem-solving. Think of it as relationship CrossFit. Sure, it's exhausting, but every argument you handle well is like adding another plate to the emotional barbell—you're building resilience as a team.

Humor can also play a role in turning arguments into bonding experiences. Let's say you're mid-debate over something trivial, like who left the lights on. Instead of escalating, you might pause and say, "You know, in the grand history of human relationships, I'm sure this is the dumbest thing two people have fought about." Sharing a laugh doesn't erase the disagreement, but it reminds you both that you're on the same side.

Arguments can also highlight your strengths as a couple. Maybe one of you is great at de-escalating tension, while the other is a pro at finding solutions. Recognizing and appreciating these complementary skills helps you tackle future conflicts with confidence. It's like being a superhero duo: one of you is the peacemaker, and the other is the strategist. Together, you're unstoppable.

That said, not every argument will feel like a bonding opportunity in the moment. Sometimes, you'll need to take a break and revisit the conversation later with cooler heads. This isn't a failure—it's a sign of maturity. Stepping away when things get too heated prevents unnecessary damage and gives both of you time to reflect. When you come back to the discussion, you're better equipped to handle it constructively.

One surprising benefit of arguments is that they often lead to greater clarity. Disagreements force you to articulate what you want, need, and value—and to hear the same from your partner. This clarity helps you avoid future conflicts and strengthens your understanding of each other. For example, after arguing about how to spend weekends, you might realize that one of you craves downtime while the other thrives on social plans. Armed with this knowledge, you can plan better in the future.

Even the process of repairing after an argument can deepen your connection. Apologizing, making amends, and working together to move forward shows that you're both committed to the relationship. It's not about avoiding conflict but about proving that your bond is stronger than any single disagreement.

Arguments also create shared stories—those moments you'll laugh about later. "Remember the time we fought about who ate the last slice of pizza?" might not seem funny at first, but give it time. These small, silly disagreements become part of your relationship's history, reminding you of how far you've come.

Ultimately, arguments are just another part of the imperfect, unpredictable journey of love. They're not signs that something is wrong—they're opportunities to learn, grow, and connect. And speaking of love, the next section will explore how to stay committed to each other, flaws and all, with lighthearted affirmations to keep your bond strong.

Lighthearted Affirmations for Staying Committed, Flaws and All

Every relationship is a package deal. You get the loving moments, the shared laughter, the adorable habits—and the quirks, flaws, and occasional toothpaste cap battles. Staying committed, flaws and all, means embracing the full reality of your partnership, not just the Instagram-worthy highlights. And sometimes, the best way to stay grounded in love is through lighthearted affirmations that remind you why you're in this together.

Here are a few to keep in your back pocket for when imperfection makes an appearance:

"I love you, even when you forget to text me back... for three hours."

This affirmation acknowledges your partner's quirks while reminding them (and yourself) that your love isn't contingent on them being perfect. Plus, it's a lot nicer than passive-aggressively forwarding your previous "Did you see this?" messages.

"Our love is stronger than your refusal to use a coaster."

Every couple has that one tiny annoyance that resurfaces no matter how many times it's addressed. Turning it into a playful affirmation transforms frustration into humor—and maybe even convinces them to grab that coaster after all.

"I choose you, even when you insist on packing five pairs of shoes for a weekend trip."

Some quirks are just part of the deal. Sure, you could grumble about the overstuffed suitcase, but isn't it more fun to laugh about it and move on? After all, you've got other things to pack—like snacks.

"I love how you make me laugh... even when we're arguing about directions."

A well-timed laugh can take the edge off almost any disagreement. This affirmation not only highlights your partner's humor but also serves as a gentle nudge to keep things light during tense moments.

"Our flaws make us a perfect fit."

This one's a classic because it's true. The little imperfections you bring to the table often complement each other in ways that make your relationship unique. Where you fall short, they step up, and vice versa.

Using affirmations like these isn't about glossing over issues or pretending everything's perfect—it's about choosing to focus on what you love and appreciate about each other. It's a reminder that love is bigger than the laundry on the floor, the dishes in the sink, or even the thermostat wars.

But affirmations aren't just about words; they're about actions, too. Back up your playful promises with small gestures that reinforce your commitment. Leave a note on the fridge that says, "Even if you forget to defrost the chicken, you're still my favorite." Or text them mid-day: "Thinking about you. Also thinking about how you load the dishwasher, but mostly you."

The beauty of lighthearted affirmations is that they reframe imperfection as something to celebrate rather than fix. They shift your perspective from, *Why do they do this?* to, *How lucky am I to share these quirks with someone I love?* They're not a cure-all for conflict, but they're a way to keep the big picture in focus, even when the small stuff gets in the way.

And when you combine affirmations with humor, they become even more powerful. Instead of letting flaws create distance, you turn them into opportunities for connection. The next time your partner does something that drives you a little nuts, try thinking of a playful affirmation that reflects your love in that moment. Who knows—it might just make you laugh instead of rolling your eyes.

Staying committed through flaws and all isn't about ignoring what's hard—it's about loving what's real. The quirks, the imperfections, the things that make your partner uniquely them—that's the stuff of true connection. And as you embrace these little idiosyncrasies, you'll find that your love becomes deeper, richer, and far more interesting than any fairytale romance.

Up next, we'll wrap up this chapter by exploring how to embrace the journey of growth together—arguments, quirks, and all—because love is as much about the journey as it is the destination.

Embracing the Journey of Growth Together, Arguments Included

Relationships are less about reaching a destination and more about the winding, unpredictable journey you take together. Along the way, you'll encounter bumps in the road, unexpected detours, and maybe even a flat tire or two. But when you embrace the journey—arguments, quirks, and all—you'll find that the twists and turns make the ride all the more meaningful.

First, let's reframe arguments as milestones instead of roadblocks. Every disagreement you navigate successfully is a step forward in your growth as a couple. Think of it this way: arguing isn't a sign that your relationship is broken; it's proof that you're both invested enough to care. When you tackle conflicts with empathy, humor, and a commitment to resolution, you're not just patching things up— you're building a stronger foundation.

Part of embracing the journey is accepting that growth is a process, not a destination. There's no magical point where you'll have "perfectly" figured out how to argue, compromise, or communicate. Instead, you'll keep learning about each other as you evolve individually and as a team. The quirks that made you laugh in year one might drive you a little crazy in year five—but that's okay. Growth means adapting to each other's changes with curiosity rather than frustration.

A sense of humor is your best companion on this journey. Let's say you've had the same argument about how to divide household chores for the fifth time. Instead of throwing up your hands in defeat, you might say, "Well, at least we're consistent!" Finding the funny side of recurring conflicts reminds you that no disagreement is bigger than your love. Plus, laughing at yourself (and each other) keeps things light enough to move forward.

Another key to embracing growth is practicing gratitude for the moments of connection along the way. Did your partner make you coffee when you had a rough morning? Acknowledge it. Did they humor you by watching your favorite show, even though they secretly hate it? Let them know you noticed. These small gestures are the glue that holds your journey together, even when the path gets rocky.

And don't forget to celebrate your wins as a couple. Maybe you finally figured out a compromise on family holiday plans, or perhaps you successfully navigated a big life decision without losing your cool. These moments deserve recognition, no matter how small. Toast to your teamwork, your resilience, and your ability to come back stronger after every disagreement.

It's also helpful to remember that every couple's journey is unique. Comparing your relationship to others—whether it's your best friend's marriage or the picture-perfect couple on Instagram—only adds unnecessary pressure. Instead, focus on the story you're writing together. It's okay if your journey looks more like a sitcom than a sweeping romance. After all, love is less about the grand gestures and more about the everyday moments of showing up for each other.

Growth also means embracing the imperfections that make your relationship real. Maybe you're both terrible at keeping track of anniversaries, or you argue about directions every time you're in the car. Instead of seeing these moments as flaws, frame them as chapters in your shared story. After all, who wants a perfectly polished romance when you can have one that's full of funny, flawed, and uniquely "you" moments?

Finally, remember that growth doesn't happen in isolation. Every argument, every compromise, every inside joke is a shared step forward. You're not just growing individually; you're growing together. And when you approach the journey with patience, humor, and a lot of love, you'll find that even the tough parts bring you closer.

As you navigate the twists and turns of your relationship, keep this in mind: love isn't about perfection—it's about persistence. It's about showing up, sticking it out, and finding joy in the messy, wonderful process of building a life together.

And with that, let's move on to the final chapter, where we'll celebrate the harmony you can find in love and conflict—because no matter what, you've got this.

Conclusion

If you've made it this far, congratulations—you've survived a deep dive into the world of arguing, compromising, and laughing your way through a relationship. By now, you've probably realized the truth: love isn't about never fighting; it's about how you fight, recover, and grow together. It's messy, it's imperfect, and at times, it's absolutely ridiculous. But it's also what makes love worth it.

Arguments are an inevitable part of any relationship, but they're not a sign of failure. In fact, they're proof that you care enough to engage. Each disagreement is a chance to learn about yourself, your partner, and the ever-changing dynamic between you. Think of them as the potholes on the road of love—they might jostle you a bit, but they don't have to derail your journey.

The beauty of relationships is that they're a constant work in progress. There's no finish line where you suddenly have everything figured out. Instead, love is about lifelong learning. Some lessons are practical, like how to communicate your needs or fold towels without triggering World War III. Others are hilarious, like the realization that your partner is physically incapable of loading the dishwasher correctly (but, bless them, they try). Every moment, from the big milestones to the smallest quirks, adds to the rich tapestry of your life together.

And let's not forget the importance of humor. If there's one thing that can save a relationship from the brink of disaster, it's the ability to laugh—at yourselves, at each other, and at the absurd situations life throws your way. Humor is the bridge between conflict and connection, a reminder that love doesn't have to be so serious all the time. Sure, you might still argue about which way the toilet paper roll goes, but isn't it better to end that fight with a laugh and a kiss than with stony silence?

As you move forward, celebrate the efforts you've made to communicate with humor and grace. It's no small feat to navigate the ups and downs of love while keeping mutual respect at the forefront. Every time you apologize sincerely, listen attentively, or find a way to laugh in the middle of a disagreement, you're strengthening the foundation of your relationship. Those little moments of connection and understanding are what make love resilient.

Remember, your relationship is uniquely yours, quirks and all. There's no need to compare it to anyone else's. What works for you might not work for your friends, and that's okay. The important thing is that you and your partner are building something that feels right for *you*. Celebrate the journey you're on together, even when it gets a little bumpy.

As you continue to grow together, hold onto these affirmations:

- Love is not about being perfect; it's about showing up, flaws and all.
- Arguments are not failures; they're opportunities to grow closer.
- Humor is not a luxury; it's a necessity.

- And most importantly, laughter and love are always worth the effort.

So here's to you and your partner—two wonderfully imperfect people navigating the chaos of life together. May your arguments be productive, your compromises creative, and your laughter endless. Keep showing up for each other, keep communicating with grace, and keep finding joy in the messy, magical journey of love.

No matter what, you've got this.

Share the Love

"Love isn't about never fighting—it's about always coming back to each other after the bell rings." – A Wise, Probably Married Person

Hey there, love sparring champ! If you've made it to this page, it means you've journeyed through the jabs, dodges, and playful grapples of *Sparring With Love*. Thank you for stepping into this quirky, imperfect ring with me and trusting me to tag along in your relationship adventures. I hope you laughed, learned, and maybe even saw your partner in a new, endearing light.

Now, I have a small favor to ask. It's not for me (okay, it's *partly* for me), but mostly for someone you don't even know yet. Someone who's currently stuck in a tag team fight over the "right" way to load the dishwasher or wondering if all those arguments mean they're doing this whole love thing wrong. Someone who needs a guide, a good laugh, and a little nudge to remind them that love is worth the sparring.

That's where you come in.

Would you leave a review?

I get it—life's busy. But hear me out. A review takes less than a minute to write and costs absolutely nothing. Yet that simple act could make all the difference for someone standing in the bookstore (or scrolling online) wondering if this book is the one that might make their next argument a little less intense—and a lot more fun.

Your review might help:

- One more couple laugh instead of stew about their quirks.
- One more person see arguments as steppingstones to growth, not landmines.
- One more partner learn that "winning" a fight isn't nearly as important as loving through it.

If this book made you laugh, gave you new tools, or simply helped you roll your eyes at your partner's quirks in a kinder way, your words could do the same for someone else.

Scan the QR code to leave your review on Amazon.

That one small gift of a review not only helps others but also keeps the love-sparring wisdom flowing to more people who could use a dose of humor and connection in their relationships.

From the bottom of my love-sparring heart, thank you for sharing your experience. You've already taken steps to make your relationship stronger—and now, you're helping others do the same.

Here's to more laughter, love, and slightly fewer arguments about thermostat settings.

Yours in playful partnership,

Avery Wells